NEW
WELSH
FICTION

Edited by Susie Wild

PARTHIAN

Parthian
The Old Surgery
Napier Street
Cardigan
SA43 1ED

www.parthianbooks.com

First published in 2014
© The Authors 2014
This collection © Parthian Books 2014
All Rights Reserved

ISBN 978-1-909844-40-7

Editor: Susie Wild

Illustrations and cover by John Abell
Cover Design by Claire Houguez
Typeset by Elaine Sharples
Printed and bound by Dinefwr Press

Published with the financial support of the Welsh Books Council

British Library Cataloguing in Publication Data

A cataloguing record for this book is available from the British Library.

This book is sold subject to the condition that it shall not by way of trade or otherwise be circulated without the publisher's prior consent in any form of binding or cover other than that in which it is published.

Stories

Onwards *Dan Tyte*	1
The Battle of St Mary Street *Robert Lewis*	7
Tomatoes *Roshi Fernando*	19
Vegetable Matters *Deborah Kay Davies*	31
Exile all the Longer *Joâo Morais*	41
My Cousin's Gun *Holly Müller*	49
Holiday of a Lifetime *Rachel Trezise*	61
Mangleface *Tyler Keevil*	75
The Bereaved *Georgia Carys Williams*	89
Diving for Starters *Siân Melangell Dafydd*	105
Sound Waves *Lane Ashfeldt*	113
Meringue *Craig Hawes*	131
Oku Hanafu *Eluned Gramich*	141
Keeper *Rebbecca Ray*	163
Disneyland *Richard Owain Roberts*	171
Into The Inwood *Rhian Edwards*	183
Moles *Monique Schwitter (trans by Eluned Gramich)*	189
Soft but Definite *Sarah Coles*	197
On Dry Land *Peter Krištúfek (trans by John Minahane)*	205
Friday *Carly Holmes*	215
Letters Home *Susmita Bhattacharya*	227
Biographies	239
Acknowledgements	249

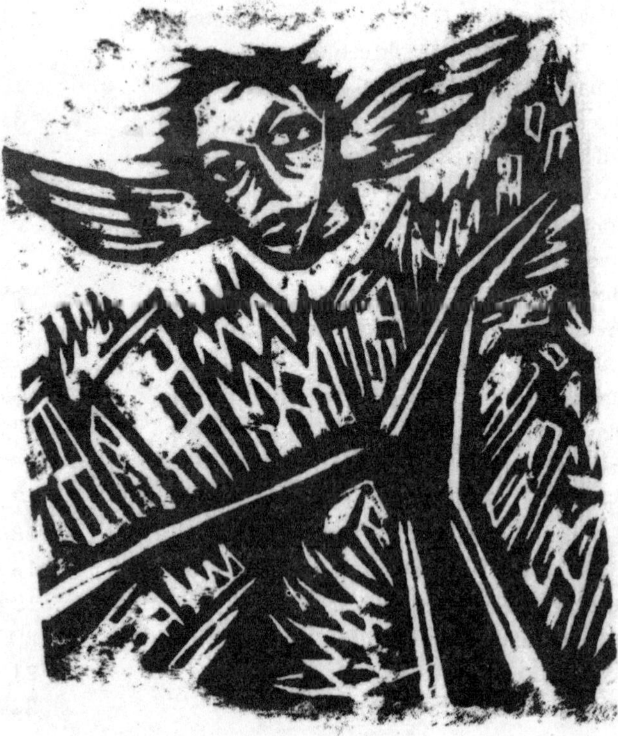

Onwards

Dan Tyte

You take a left at the bar nobody could ever remember the name of, the one where the waiting girl wore her hair up and her guard down, where the pool table sloped into the top right pocket and the sharks circled for fresh blood till Vince called time every night by shutting the jukebox off, switching the lights on and insisting you got the hell out. Past the blood that still stains the pavement from when Jimmy Jones floored Tommy Tyler with a cold hard right after an argument over a girl or a gun or a girl and a gun. Keep going right on past there till you come to the little shop where Mr Aaronson and Mr Aaronson before him and Mr Aaronson before him sweltered in the tight kitchen under the heat of the furnace that baked the bagels in the small hours before the dawn to feed the workers who would wait outside his door before the shift started in the factory two doors down. Then head under the iron bridge whose blue paint peels under the weight of the misguided ones that ride the rail on a one-way ticket out of town which they all come to regret, some sooner, some later. Take the second right and the street, much wider now, is where the museum and the city hall sit like sphinxes, aloof and aware, perched on Portland stone steps. At the bottom of the steps, slide past the spot where the politicians electioneer under April skies, making promises that we've heard same place, different time, and you'll come to the park. The lungs of the city they call it, the place where teenagers tearaway and drink the first drink and old men fall away and drink the last. A green felt where sweethearts stroll and squabble and kiss and make up and make plans. Where dogs bark and bounce after balls and perverts prowl and camouflage filthy thoughts and dirty desires with nightfall or foliage. Keep on going straight past the place where the self-proclaimed Pied Piper left the decapitated body of 17-year-old Janie Jeffries, the first of six that mad hot Seventies summer that left the police dancing to his tune until he made the fatal mistake of letting on his first name and the call was traced to his mother's apartment where the SWAT bust in and bust him before locking him up and swallowing the key. Then take a sharp right and you'll come to the narrow lanes lined with market stalls, where you can shut your eyes and the shouts of the scalpers and the smells of the spices, and the cobbles under your soles let you know that you could be nowhere on earth but where you are right now and where you want to be always. Fire ahead five hundred yards past the labour exchange where in the thirties the flat caps filled the floor outside and grey sallow men shrunk against the brickwork and filed down back the way you came. Follow your nose until you smell the fine food from the kitchen of The Ritz, where good men become bad men and city officials are served brown envelopes for dessert. You'll then come to a fork in the road, as we often do, and you need to take a left, staying close to the trees that line the kerb. You're now at the spot the tour guides say gives the best shot of the tallest tower in the city. But I'm no tour guide. Shoot straight on past where the newspapers roll off the presses and into the waiting vans and onto the hands of the sports fans and stock market. Left at the place where they say the first brick of the city was laid all those years ago by men – it was always men in those days – with lofty ideas and clinical naivety. If only they could see what they'd begun. You're now on the route taken by the Lord Mayor's Parade, where the Africans shake the stigma off and smile like they don't live in the bad part of town and can't afford to put the heating on tonight while the beauty queen waves from an open top car wondering if she'll ever know love like this again. It's the same road where the local sports team celebrated after they got a last-minute cup final winner against that team from the other city a half hour up the road but a million miles away from here. Left again at the boarded-up library onto the man-made district where concrete becomes cardboard, the cold bites hard and eyes are averted and the city subverted, at least until the corner is turned to the tracks where the trams used to run and the rattle of their rails could be heard a mile or more down the winding line kidding you into thinking it'd be with you sooner than it ever was. Bear right along where the picket line was made by brave men with morals and appetites and broken by them with worries and wives and the community split and the fault lines still flail. Bend around past the terraced red-brick houses where the truants once knocked doors and ran and now make scores in gangs. Skim through the still-stumbling streets where the warning sounded and the sirens whirred and all you could smell was the smoke and the search for the answer. Down along where the rain ran for one hundred days straight in '67 or '68 and the flood waters didn't wait for an invitation to tea. Up the path which hummed of the hops boiled in towers of the brewery which quenched the city before it closed down. Onwards, always onwards. And then it's there, on your right. You can't miss it. Or ever forget it.

This is your city now.

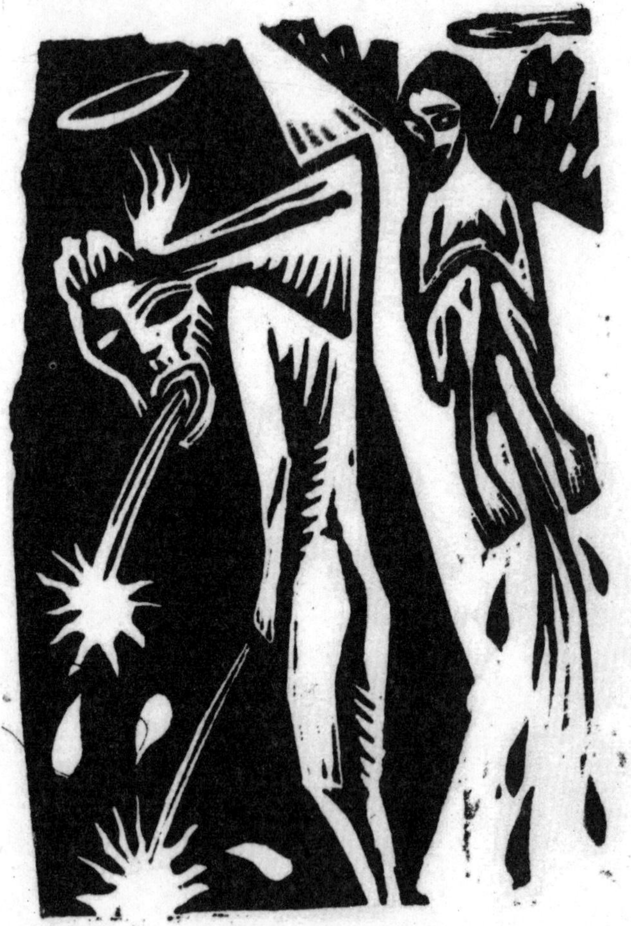

The Battle of St Mary Street

Robert Lewis

Somewhere a little up ahead came the sound of a small, wet explosion, and, not long after, Smithy bent double, clutching his stomach, and slid to the ground. Their unit had been advancing up the street, keeping close to the buildings, stepping over the bodies, hugging cover. When Smithy fell, they ducked instinctively into the nearest doorway and crouched there, out of the line of sight.

Around them the once-friendly city was a glade of shadows, shrouded in smoke and darkness and screams. Silhouettes slipped stumbling through the fog like spectres, in loose groups or in haunting solitude; they appeared briefly and were gone, collateral damage, you could call it, the walking wounded of an unwinnable war. What they had lost, what they were searching for, could only be guessed at. Somewhere behind them came the rumble of a fast-moving convoy, hurtling unseen towards some urgent destination. Up ahead a warning siren Dopplered in and out and ever more slowly away.

Simmons, on his hands and knees, craned his neck around the doorway as near to street level as he could.

'Looks like his guts are shot,' he said.

None of them made any move to help him. When your guts went like that, there was nothing you could do. And anyway, it was Smithy who was the first-aider. For what good it did any of them. Three days' residential training at headquarters in Basingstoke was what it amounted to. Coffee and Bourbons and a few goes trying to resuscitate a plastic torso with your fists. It was a joke. It was all a joke.

A moment's silent reverence fell upon them and Shenkins called out back down the street.

'Tina? Davey? Tina?'

There was no answer.

'Stop it ducks,' said the oldest of them. 'You'll draw attention to us.'

In between Simmons and Shenkins, Gabby Pritchard sat cross-legged rolling a cigarette, her back pressed up against the glass. Single, late thirties, a data-entry supervisor unprepossessing in looks and attitude, nobody had ever given much thought to plain Jane Pritchard in more peaceful times. But now you could see something solid about her, something that if not exactly reassuring was at least resigned.

The mouse had become a rock. She had never spoken about it, but her two young colleagues looked at her and saw just from the lines of her face that she had been here before. Here was what you called veterancy: experience survived.

In the darkness between them a lighter flashed, and was followed by the slow pulsing glow of a cigarette.

'I don't even know where we're supposed to be going,' said Simmons, still on his hands and knees, his voice cracking.

'I think Debs said it was Revolution,' said Shenkins.

Pritchard laughed, a deep tarry sound, at some private joke.

'Revolution,' she repeated. 'It's not Revolution. It's the same every year.'

Shenkins pulled the Nokia out of her jacket and keyed in a couple of numbers. The phone shook in her hand.

'She's not answering.'

'Try Tanya.'

'None of them are answering. Nobody.'

'Do you think they made it?' asked Simmons.

'Who knows.'

'Maybe we're the last ones left,' said Simmons, that crack in his voice still there, and widening. 'I don't even know where we are.'

Shenkins put her phone back into her jacket pocket, after dropping it a few times, and squinted at the dark wooden board high-up above them.

'I think it used to be a Hard Rock Cafe,' she said. 'I wonder where Jones-Cavendish is?'

'You know bloody well where he is,' coughed Gabby Pritchard. 'In the front room of some five-bedroomed house in the Vale with his family, spread on a leather three-piece, watching the flat screen. Wife in the kitchen. Children playing on the rug. Bowl of peanuts on one side of him and a glass of cab sav on the other. Two cars in the driveway. Somewhere nice and quiet and warm. Miles away from here.'

Jones-Cavendish had got them all in the meeting room that afternoon and handed out the staff gift parcels. Shenkins had got a ten pound Tesco voucher and a bottle of Fructis shampoo. She didn't know what everyone else got. Then he had told them to knock-off half an hour early, to have a few for him, to enjoy themselves, 'to do us proud'.

'See you next year,' he'd said, and it was the last they'd seen of him.

She wondered where her Fructis shampoo was now. Somewhere under the seats in the Prince of Wales with her scarf and her gloves and her coat. With everything and everyone else they had already lost and left behind. So much, so many, already gone. Some hadn't been able to cope with the pressure, and had sacrificed themselves the first chance they'd got.

Shenkins remembered Gavin Bowen, a gentle alternative-looking type who wore stringy ties and had thick-framed glasses, one of the young team leaders they'd brought in at the end of November. She had stood behind him and watched him spend that Friday morning sending emails of love and apology to friends and family. When they had piled out of the taxis by Walkabout he had been part of the first wave, had hit the crowd running and made the bar, had got a round of fourteen tequilas in but then drank them all himself. He never made it out. It was as if he had wanted to die.

Shenkins drew her knees up to her chin and wrapped her arms around herself. Although she couldn't feel it, she knew she was very, very cold. Through the frosted mist she could see could see the traffic lights at Wood Street turning from red to green. No traffic passed. Wood Street. Christ. They were still at the bottom of St Mary Street. They had advanced about sixty or seventy yards, and it had cost them – what had it cost them? She opened her purse. The better part of two days, at four ninety three an hour.

Simmons descended into a coughing fit that sent him sprawling onto his side. When it ended his mouth continued to spasm open and shut, his face creased with some unknown emotion.

'I don't even know what we're doing here,' he sobbed. Or maybe it was laughter. It was impossible to tell.

Gabby Pritchard sucked deep on her cigarette, stubbed it out onto the tiles, and stood up. She was remarkably steady.

'We're here because it's Christmas,' she said. 'Somewhere. Now only two kinds of people are going to stay on this street. Those who have passed out on it, and those who are going to pass out. Get on your feet.'

With one hand on the door frame for support, Jane Shenkins climbed to the top of her four-inch heels. Neil Simmons was still unable to get up from all fours, so they lifted him, slowly, like you would with an old dog whose back legs had gone. Once he was upright he could more or less stand on his own.

'It's up from down, is what it is,' he explained. 'How I remember is that down hurts and up just sort of strains.'

Up ahead they caught up with Smithy, curled in a

foetal position near an impressive pool, no, a reservoir, of his own vomit, like a quotation mark around a speech bubble.

'We can't leave him here,' said Shenkins.

Gabby Pritchard was unmoved.

'Well we can't carry him. Put him up against the wall there and we'll put something on top of him, keep him warm.'

In the end they covered him in bulging black bin bags from outside of the Spar and cordoned him off with four traffic cones. Shenkins didn't feel bad about it. She had looked into his eyes, cold and glassy and distant, like coins at the bottom of some well, and seen he was at peace.

For the living there was only this – this – what could you call it, Jane Shenkins wondered? A party? No, it was nothing as coherent as that. A celebration? Certainly not. There was nothing being honoured here, nothing kept. What were they doing? Spending money they didn't really have with people that weren't really friends.

They weren't rebelling, no way, they were doing exactly what was expected of them, really. And did any of them even want the same thing, did it occur to them that maybe they even wanted anything? No, they weren't rebels. They would come out, clog up the bars and the streets and the emergency wards, and then they would disappear again, and nothing would change. They were insurgents. Like in Iraq.

The possibility stopped her in her tracks. She tugged at Gabby's sleeve with an expression of awestruck wonderment.

'This is an insurgency,' she said. Gabby, too, stopped. The features of her face grew concerned.

'Do you need a piss love? We can go in The Borough.'

'No!' she screamed, but no one heard. Maybe she never said it out loud. That was more her style, after all, to scream inside.

'Come on,' said Gabby, an arm around her shoulder, steering her towards another densely packed crowd, another beery throng that would suck them up and contain them the way aspic does with meat chunks. And it might hold them trapped like that forever, or at least until somebody rang the bell and the whole thing disintegrated.

Only at the threshold did she bridle.

'Come on,' said Gabby, pushing her forward. 'It's freezing and I need to pay a visit myself. Come on.'

'Why?' she blurted, suddenly conscious that in the last few minutes, or the last few hours, who knows, she had regressed to some form of helpless, pouting infancy. There didn't seem anything she could do about it.

'Look,' said Gabby. 'This is it. This is what we've got. A couple of hours, is all. And then it's "Gabby, have you got a stapler?" and "Oh, I Tippexed my name on the bottom and you've still got my stapler". Let yourself go. Have some fun. A little bit of adventure, hey? Don't worry. We'll all be back there soon enough. Just give yourself something to a laugh about hey? When we're back. The stories they'll tell, hey? The stories they'll tell. Now. Here. Put your reindeer antlers on.'

And even then, perhaps, Jane Shenkins might yet have balked at the final hurdle, might have strolled off to

Charlotte Street for some chips, and caught her bus. If she'd left then, she could probably have still made it on under her own steam. But Neil Simmons, the wobbling Neil Simmons, teetering like a tree that didn't know it had been felled, swooped towards the doorway in a dive, and the crowd swallowed him up and he was gone. And so they followed on, into the breach.

And then, who knows, stuff happened. She drank something that was on fire. She drank something that wasn't on fire. She tried to buy a drink with a Tesco voucher. The pub rocked excitingly from side to side, like the pirate ship in a fairground. At times the crowd would bunch and keep you steady, other times it would part and you'd be hurtling across the room like a knocked skittle. She tried to go the toilets but couldn't manage it somehow – there was some minor logistical difficulty; it was locked, or it was a cupboard. When she came back Gabby Pritchard had little Neil Simmons on her knee like a ventriloquist's dummy, and their tongues were mashing furiously together like sea anemones.

She watched them briefly for a moment, the horror, the horror, and somehow she was released. She was outside. Not free yet though; there was something she had to do. She found herself crossing the street, and squatting down between the cash points, which seemed like a logical spot at the time, a blast of cold air hitting her thighs and her buttocks as she rolled her tights down to her ankles and she remembered oh yes, yes, it was this. And she was, she supposed, ashamed, in some numb and distant way, in some manner now theoretical and abstract and much removed. But it wouldn't take long.

Then she pulled up her tights and got them most of the way up, fell over, and cried.

Her legs were wet now. She could feel it. Even so, she didn't cry for long. It wasn't like it used to be, when you would cry and mam or dad or Aunty Sheel would come and see to you. You cried now, and well, you just cried. She stopped crying and decided she was tired and she needed a rest and she slumped ever nearer to the horizontal. In the end her head came to rest against a black metal box that was fastened to the wall and overflowing with receipts. And from that fixed position her gaze fell on a purple flyer on the pavement.

'Our products make people look gorgeous. That makes me feel great too,' said Katarzyna, Store Colleague at Boots.

Be part of a magical team this Christmas.

Christmas at Boots is a very exciting time and we'll look to you to make our customers feel special by providing such a fantastic shopping experience they'll want to hurry back soon.

'There was such a buzz, and it was incredibly busy,' said Zineb, a Team Manager.

Bring your sparkle to our stores this Christmas. A typical day will involve activities, from keeping shelves stocked and displays looking vibrant, to spotting opportunities for linked sales and increasing loyalty wherever you can. You'll need to be helpful in a natural and friendly way making sure every customer you meet leaves the store feeling delighted with the care and attention you have given them.'

Be part of a magical team this Christmas. Ha. She had

been part of a magical Christmas team once, all of them together, and hardly any shouting she could remember. She had made presents for her mother and her father and her sister and her brother and her aunt, and made them entirely herself, not the presents the teacher got you to make at school. She'd got the ideas out of *Bunty*. She must have been about seven, she supposed. She tried to remember Christmas Eve when she was seven and found much to her surprise that she could.

She had shared a room with her sister, and their little brother was sleeping that night on a camp bed between them because Aunty Sheel had his room, and their father had come in and read to them a story about a Gingerbread Man to help them get to sleep. A man who'd never read a book in his life. It had been nice, then. And if Jane Shenkins had retained any basic motor control of her face, she would have smiled.

Over the road the pub was still full of people. The street was full of people now too. She wished her tights were on properly. She wished she wasn't sitting in her own piss. She wondered, vaguely, if she was still wearing her reindeer antlers.

She imagined Gabbie Pritchard and Neil Simmons in The Borough pub and waited for them to come out. They didn't come out.

The stories they'll tell, she could hear Gabbie Pritchard nudging her, the stories they'll tell.

And realisation came upon Jane Shenkins fast and clear, as if she was sober as a stone. That when you grew up, you didn't want to tell stories any more, but pretend you were in them. And on Black Friday in St Mary Street,

Cardiff, this seemed to her then the root of all misery in the whole, twisted war-ridden world.

And soon after, when they came for her, in their high visibility jackets, working their way up the street like bin men, when she was received, once more, into the arms of policemen and ambulance men and the ambivalent benevolence of the state, she was crying again. But with an adult's grief.

Because she knew, of this rare lesson, she would remember nothing.

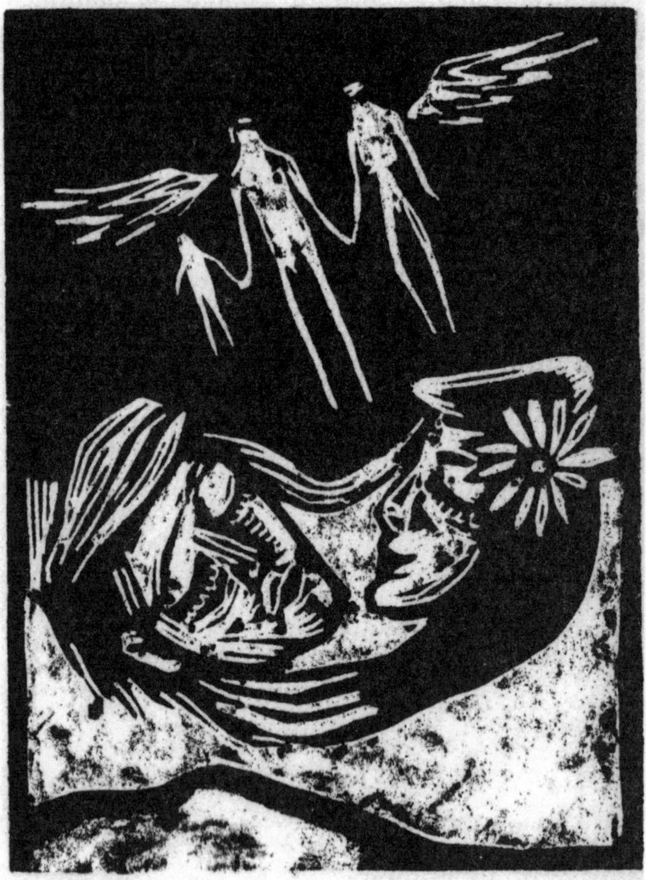

Tomatoes

Roshi Fernando

Joyce was staring through the back window of the narrow kitchen, at the washing dancing on the line – all the little whites, vests and nappies – brilliant in the sunshine. They were a reminder of her long ago, lost now. All those days of nappies boil-washed on the stove after she'd wrapped one or other of her babies in a hand-knitted shawl and put them in the big pram in the garden. Sashi followed her gaze:

'David, oh God, the washing – I said to bring it in,' and David ran out, as if it were normal, though he had done a full day at work and Sashi had been at home with the birthday boy. Joyce winced: she hated to see her son servile, and particularly, to this woman, this girl who trapped him with a pregnancy.

When Joyce was five, she was evacuated to Llangadog, and lived on a farm near an army base. There had been black Americans there, and the farm girls had dated them and one had fallen pregnant.

'We used to wonder,' she said to Sashi once, 'if the babies would come out stripy. I wonder if your baby will come out stripy?' she had said, idly laughing, sipping tea in David's back garden. It was *his* back garden. He had inherited the money for the house from Joyce's great aunt. It was *his*.

The child, Tom, was three today. Little fellow, charmingly curly haired and pale: the only intimation of darkness his hooded eyes. Like an Arab, Joyce had said to her daughter Ellen. Ellen had told her to hush, it was so rude.

'You're so old-fashioned, Mother.' Ellen's son Andrew was blonde, nearly six, perfect in every way, except his parents had divorced and he was now so timid, Joyce hardly heard his voice from one week to the next. Tom, on the other hand, articulated grandiloquent words: dinosaur names and sentences of refusal so persuasive it was difficult not to fall head over heels. But somehow she resisted. She would put him on her lap, and he would do his best to charm, and she would admonish him, because it was good for him, and good for Sashi to understand motherhood was not about making the child happy. Motherhood was – well, it was harder than that.

She watched David carry the carefully folded nappies in from the garden in a wicker basket.

'Come on Mum. Come outside. It's beautiful. Tom

wants to show you his sandpit. Dad's got his shoes and socks off already. I'm going to get my camera.'

'It's time that child was out of nappies,' she said. Then: 'How's the vegetable patch coming?'

David was silent. He put the basket down in the hallway and came back into the sitting room. He took his camera from a shelf behind Joyce. He looked down at her as he stretched. She smiled at him. He went outside. Joyce sat at the dining table, waiting.

* * *

Roberto rang the bell. He held Andrew's hand, and a football wrapped in birthday paper covered in balloons. Ellen stood behind them, carrying a plate of sandwiches and a bottle of wine. Joyce answered the door.

'Andrew! Darling!' she said, quite loudly. Roberto felt the child's hand tighten around his own. He squeezed it and they stood still for a moment. Roberto looked in past Joyce's shoulder. From the doorway, he could see through into the dark kitchen and out into the back garden. There were Sashi's family sitting on a circle of plastic chairs. Her father, her mother, one of Sashi's aunts.

'Hello Andrew,' Sashi called from the top of the stairs. 'I'm just changing Tom. He's desperate to see you!' Roberto could see Sashi's legs.

'Hi, hi,' Ellen shouted back. 'Andrew's got you something.'

'Andrew!' he heard the child shout. It sounded perfect in his voice, the name. Roberto removed Andrew's jacket with his left hand, pulling at the back of the collar, while still holding the child. Roberto understood Andrew's fear of his grandmother.

'Come on,' he whispered. 'We go in the garden.'

Sashi brought Tom downstairs. Ellen kissed her on both cheeks, swept Tom up into the air, back down again for a cuddle and a kiss. She had been talking to Joyce, but stopped mid-flow.

'Joyce, come and see my tomatoes,' Sashi said linking her arm to her mother-in-law's and walking her outside.

Tom struggled from Ellen's arms. He stood in the midst of the legs and clapped his hands for joy: he looked to Andrew and Roberto, and to Sashi's parents.

'Seeya!' he called to Sashi's father 'Look! Andrew!' and he presented the five-year-old to them all with his palms turned upward, as if pushing forward a plate of delights. Andrew dropped to his knees in front of the child, and Tom ran to him, placed his hands about the older boy's face and kissed him on both cheeks, on the nose. He said

'Andrew. Andrew. Andrew, come and see, come and see.' The two children walked to the end of the long garden, around a bush, and disappeared. And there was silence, and the groups of adults looked at one another, Sashi and Joyce to David's father sitting on the ledge of the shell shaped sandpit, Roberto to Sashi's father and mother smiling quietly toward the empty space where the children had been, and David to Sashi, to her face, to her beautiful face.

* * *

Just outside Rome, there is a piece of land, near a spring where Roberto's father collected his weekly supply of drinking water. It's a small piece Roberto's father had bought from a farmer. He liked to grow his own vegetables. For years, since Roberto was a boy, they would spend Saturday morning there. When he was older, Roberto would go into the woodland at the back of the land and hunt for mushrooms. You could walk up into hills, see mountains a remarkable distance away. He tramped through thyme, through heathers. The rabbits he trapped were already steeped in aromatics. He asked his father then – *if you cut me open, would I taste of this hill?* His father chuckled – *you smell of it now* he said, smacking the back of Roberto's head with his rough, fat hand. There was always the smell of tomato stalks on his fingers: astringent, bitter, lemony. When he cooked tomato sauce with the small grape-like red droplets that grew in abundance on that Roman earth, his father could not be bothered to rip each one off the green mesh, but dropped in whole strings, stalks and all, and the sauce tasted of bitterness and history. It tasted of a past Roberto felt in the weight of the earth clogging his shoes.

Ellen sat with him next to her father on the ground. Roberto looked at the earth in this garden, looked toward the end wall, a hundred yards away perhaps. It was a long garden for such a small house, and someone had made an effort with it twenty years or so ago if you looked at the planting: there was a laid out path meandering through it, and by its side shrubs and fruit trees which had bent with the weather and looked old and worn with life. To the left was a different pathway, and he stood to watch the children play near the vegetable beds, pretending to stretch his legs. Around him he heard the older generation chatter – Ellen's mother talking of her grandsons, and her father ask a question of Sashi's father.

Roberto stood with his hands on his hips. His English was still hesitant, and Sashi had been helping him: he had spent a few afternoons with her, digging the vegetable beds, planting the tomatoes a few months ago.

'I will see the kids,' Roberto said, and he walked away from the conversation, around the corner to the children. They were playing with the large spade he would use to dig the beds – Tom picked it up and dragged it as Andrew feverishly clumped handfuls of dirt and let it crumble. They were at the beginning of something, although they had not communicated it to one another yet. They were about to explode into something, Roberto could see, and so he walked past them and beyond them, to inspect the tall tomatoes.

* * *

After they had cut the cake and Sashi's mother had taken her sister off to the shops nearby, the grownups went inside to sit in the shade. The two grandfathers took the easy chairs and settled to nap. Joyce stood at the washing up bowl while Ellen chatted. Sashi stayed in the garden with David. David sat upright on the blanket, and Sashi leaned against him. Joyce watched them through the window:

'Why,' she said quietly to Ellen.

'Really, I don't want to hear anymore,' Ellen said. 'Look at Tom. Look at what she has given you. What is wrong with you?'

'You won't even let me start to speak,' Joyce said.

'No.'

'Roberto,' Joyce said then.

'No.'

Roberto was with the children behind the bushes. They had been very quiet for half an hour at least.

'Perhaps you should check the children?' Joyce said.

'Why?'

Why indeed. Joyce looked at her son and his wife. When she was a child, she had had an atlas and that is all she would have known of where this woman was from. An atlas and perhaps some black and white photographs of the natives waving at our Queen. And now, here Sashi sat, in the middle of their family, causing happiness, causing love, as if it were entirely normal. Joyce plunged her hand into the glinting soapy water and took a champagne glass out to rinse under the tap, but she did it clumsily, her hand shaking accidentally, and it broke, and it cut her, and the blood from her finger ran down with the water. She watched it, watched it flow. She watched it carefully. Ellen had gone out to the back garden and the sunshine. Joyce realised she must clear the glass, but for a moment, she was a child again and she didn't know what to do. Tears came: she wanted to cry out. She looked about and found kitchen towels and a supermarket bag and a plaster in a drawer. She bustled and was busy, and the feeling of helplessness passed.

* * *

Roberto woke because something bounced on his face. Then another thing, and another. He recognised the smell. Tomatoes. Tomatoes as small as marbles pouring onto his face. Andrew stood over him, and Tom on the other side, framed in his aviators. They laughed and the balls bounced again onto his face. Through the green-grey lenses, he reached up and grabbed their hands.

'No, no,' he said. '*Basta!*'

The children laughed more, pulled their hands away and ran. Roberto sat up. Around his head were deep-green-streaked globules like un-burst bubbles. He picked one up, bit it, and its dryness hurt his cracked lip.

'Andrew!' he shouted after them. 'No more.' He heard his voice echo off the back red-brick wall.

'What is it?' Ellen called.

'Nothing,' he shouted back, and he heard his voice clearly, its elongated 'o' wrong. He heard David shout, 'Tom! Want some cake?' Roberto lay back down, putting his head carefully where it had been before, and he felt around the top of his head, took the balls of flesh and rubbed them into his hair, rubbed the leaves between his fingers, closed his eyes and pulled the pungent air into him. The sun was hot.

* * *

Joyce went out to say goodbye to the children. David and Ellen were making more tea and Sashi was in the sitting room, talking to her father and father-in-law. The way she sat on the arm of the sofa, her right hand on her father's shoulder, it annoyed Joyce: though she could see something in the gesture – the way the girl pulled playfully at a curl at the back of her father's head to emphasise the point – she could see an unsteadiness that was touching.

'Where are you Andrew?' she called. 'Andrew, darling.'

She walked through to the vegetable patches, and the Italian, the young fellow Ellen was dating, was down on his haunches, gathering up something, picking, like picking strawberries, one into the hand, then another, pushing the first back with the same movement. It reminded her of the farm girls, the way they weeded, squatting down here and there; it reminded her of being young in the warmth of an English summer, always summer, in her childhood.

'What have you got?' she asked him. He showed her a handful of tomatoes.

'Oh dear,' she said. She could not quite understand them in the palm of his hand. They were so small, so palely green, some of them, like the colour of a blouse or a blancmange. Not a tinge of orange or red, and when she took one gently from his palm: hard, the little thing between her fingers, like a seashell or a rock, like a fossil. She pressed her fingers firmly against the skin until a nail broke through, and she smelled the tomato-ness. She put it to her nose, and sniffed it. Roberto put his hand to his nose and sniffed too. Tom ran to her and threw his arms about her knees:

'Andrew picked tomatoes, Grandma.'

'I see,' she said. She was not sure if she should allow anger to rise, if she should use a growl in her voice. 'Did you pick the tomatoes too?'

'No,' he said solemnly, looking up to her with his huge eyes. 'It naughty.' And then he kissed her knees. 'Kisses!' he shouted triumphantly. It brought her down. She knelt to him and pulled him to her. 'No, Grandma, no!' he bellowed, and laughing, he ran away. She wiped her eyes on her arm.

'Come,' Roberto said. 'Come,' and he led her to the tomato plants. Roberto began to pinch out the suckers, and she became absorbed in the task, pulling at stringy arms and branches, showing them to Roberto, and if he nodded, breaking them off, and making a pile on the grass.

'Naughty Grandma,' Tom said. And she said:

'Yes, Grandma is very naughty, isn't she?' And she blew him a kiss.

Andrew watched Roberto, and as the pile of tomato branches grew, he busied himself with cutting and chopping and making pies and a stove in the sandpit. As he presented each adult with a tomato and sand pie, Andrew put a green cherry on the top, and when the pie for Tom was presented, they put three birthday tomatoes on and Tom blew them off and they rolled into the grass. Joyce watched them from the shade of the vegetable beds, even laughing as Tom put a green tomato onto his head, balancing it so carefully, his eyes crossed in concentration.

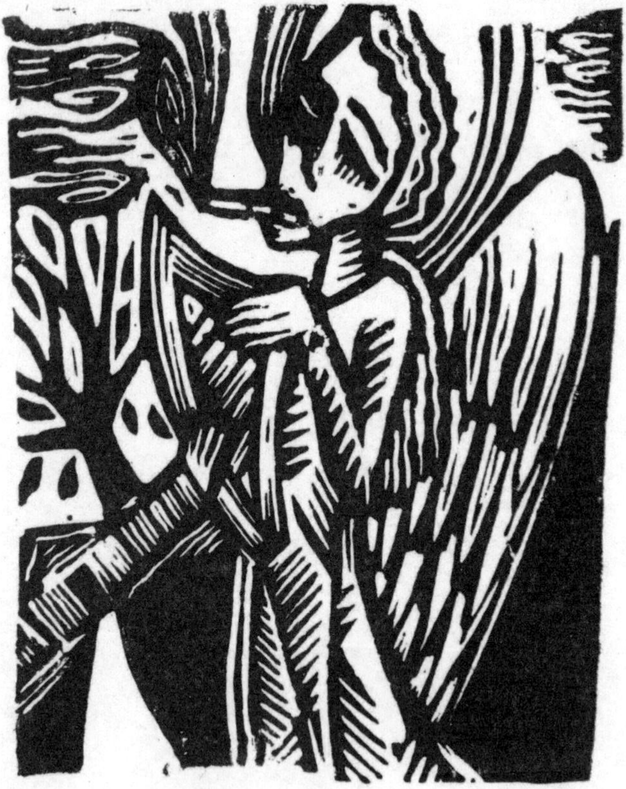

Vegetable Matters

Deborah Kay Davies

My mother always brings the conversation round to the vegetables for sale in her local market. Today I mention I've been shopping. She narrows her eyes and asks, did I buy potatoes? Then she wants to know how much I paid for them. For God's sake, Mother, I answer, who cares? She does, though, and won't be put off. How much did you cough up? she asks. Then she puts her hands on her hips. And don't bring God into this, young lady, she says. There's never an excuse for blasphemy. The Lord's name means a lot to me, even if some people I could mention have turned their backs on Him. He's guided me through many a dark valley, I can tell you. She says this mildly. It's an old argument. Mother got religion years ago. It's explained the world to her. Supplied an angel-strewn landscape for her to stroll in when things in this vale of tears got too much. Religion made it easy for her to understand people; you're either one of the many lost or one of the blessedly few found.

I begin making up stupid prices for my veg. What? How much did I pay for this magnificent swede? Five pounds Mother, and I consider that a fair price. She sniffs, unmoved. Anyway, she says, the potatoes in the market are beauties. You can do anything with them. Anything? I say, unable to stop myself. On she goes. Boil, roast, cream, she says. And they make lovely chips. And cheap? I should say so. It's all right for you, she says, jutting her chin out. But those of us living on a limited income have to count the cost. I bet you don't even know how much you pay for a bag of Granny Smiths. Dunno, I answer. Her jaw drops open on its hinge. I can almost hear the clang. Now I am truly shocked, she says. They see you coming, my girl. You're being had on a daily basis. I pick up a mottled banana from the fruit bowl. And while we're on the subject, where do you suggest I stuff this single, whopping banana, Mumsie? First you can wash your mouth out with soap and water, you rude madam, she says calmly. I'm going to put the kettle on. Over the sound of the kettle filling I can hear her sending up what she calls a little bullet prayer on my behalf.

While she's shuffling about in the kitchen I pick up *The Countryman* and leaf through it. There's an article on, surprise, surprise, root vegetables. Another on aphids. Then badgers. Then blacksmithing. Then a day in the life of a charcoal-maker. I stop at a section called 'Poetry Corner'. There's a lot of poetry about spring. Words like 'harbinger', 'glorious' and 'awakening' pop up regularly in each poem. Around the verse-edges grow little clumps of snowdrops and enormous, out-of-scale daffodils. All the reading material in my mother's house has the same effect on me. I feel an uncomfortable mixture of nostalgia and impatience, and it makes me prowl around a lot, searching in her old jars and cupboards for I don't know what.

On the surface of the dresser there's a sort of shrine-arrangement. Black and white photos of my brother and me in our Sunday best. He's squinting and I'm baring my teeth. I look at the shelves above the gas-fire. There are neat rows of photographs. Lots of ugly couples smiling toothily, their spectacles blank. They all seem to be dressed in fashions from the seventies. Large numbers of children with bulbous, spotted foreheads cluster round their knees. The children hold white bibles in their little hands. I call to my mother, who the hell are all these revolting people? Missionaries, dear, she answers. They look as if their diet is deficient in something, I say, as she comes in with a battered tray. And they're all wearing Crimplene. Clear the table, she says. Don't be so useless.

She picks up one of the photographs and studies it. Deficient in something? she muses, her lips a wavy line. Her eyes beadily search for clues. I wonder how they get their veg in those foreign places, she says under her breath. Doesn't the Lord provide? I say, and start to pour the tea. It's black and thick. Now, I'm glad you brought that to my attention, my mother says, putting the photograph down. It's a continual source of wonder and joy to me when the Lord is graciously willing to use even the most unprepossessing vessel to be the conduit of His will. I think about being a conduit while I sip my tea.

She pulls a little book out of her apron pocket. From a drawer she fishes out a pencil and licks its tip before she starts writing. I'll make a note of that and bring it up as a matter for prayer at the next missionary meeting. She starts to write, saying aloud; our brothers and sisters in the field, re: diet. If they're in the field, I say, can't they plant stuff? Anyway, none of them looks particularly thin to me. More puffy perhaps. And sweating. Well, what do you expect? Mother says. We're all still hampered with these vile bodies, and they will perspire, it's only human. I suppose even you know it's hot overseas. Seem to be having a lot of S – E – X though, I say, if you look at the shoals of kids. And in spite of all that crimp and vileness and sweat.

After we've drunk our tea she asks me if I'll stay for lunch. I know she wants to cook for me so I say yes. You sit there and relax, she says, read some magazines. I'm going to get cracking. She turns in the kitchen doorway. There are some lovely testimonies in some of those periodicals. You know, about young people who thought they didn't need God until he stepped into their lives and transformed them. Then, she says, ticking things off on her fingers, we've got carrots, cauli, broccoli, peas, swede, potatoes (roast and mashed), chicken, gravy and stuffing. Lovely, I say, and sink into my chair. But don't give me a huge amount will you? I know she'll ignore me.

In the magazine rack are various missionary leaflets. They have names like London Outreach, The Reaper's Reward, China Fields, Lost and Found. All the missionary-workers' photographs look the same. I compare them with the snaps on my mother's shelf; they're interchangeable. In amongst this stuff is something that looks like a small newspaper. It's a Jehovah's Witness handout. On the front cover there is a coloured drawing of a family. The children cuddle lambs and lion cubs. Around the woman's leg some sort of purple snake twines lovingly. The father beams down on his family. His cupped hands hold two peaceful scorpions. In the distance there's a shining city on a hill. I shout to my mother, why are you reading this JW stuff? She comes to the kitchen door holding a ladle. Know your enemy, she says, and fades back into the steam. I can hear saucepan lids rattling.

Mother stands to say grace before we eat. It goes on and on. She prays for those far from the fold and appeals to God's infinite love. I watch her salivating as she prays, but she will not cut her prayer short. It has to have three main points. Amen, I say at last. My mound of cauliflower can barely hold its shape on the plate. I touch it with my fork. It collapses. The broccoli florets are khaki. They lie across my dish like minuscule, waterlogged trees. Strangely, the swede stays in hard, orange lumps. Weirdly, I love it all.

Mother asks about my latest male friend. That's what she calls them; Your-latest-male-friend. Has he got a job? 'Yet' hangs in the air, merging with the smell of carrots. He's over-qualified, I say. Actually, it's only been six weeks, I say. This conversation is as old as my mother's Constable-country place mats. It wouldn't do for him to waste his talents, I say. What would those be then? Mother asks, and spoons a dripping pile of chicken and stuffing into her mouth. Your father's always busy, she says, chewing. First in that factory. Now looking after me. She bites into a pendulous carrot. Seen me through three breakdowns, bless him. The energy he's spent building up his little carpentry business. And people come round for him to sharpen their lawnmower blades all the time. I wouldn't be surprised if, when he arrives in Glory, he'll get himself a little job up there, fixing things. Of course, the Lord's got a soft spot for carpenters. Your father loves to serve, she says, scraping the last of the gravy off her plate with her knife and licking it clean. It's a gift, serving is. And your father and I are both blessed with it. People often comment. I'll put the kettle on. I expect you'll want coffee.

I think about my father. How he spends so much time out in his shed. How, years ago, he and I would whisper at tea time, arranging to meet later in his warm little creosote-impregnated workshop, the sweet curls of shaved wood ankle-deep on the floor. Me doing a jigsaw puzzle while he sanded down some beautiful, useless object. The feeling of being barricaded in. Rain pooling on the roof. Well, she says, patting her stomach, I believe I'll make your latest male-friend situation a matter for prayer. He is not a situation, Mother, I say. You make him sound like a hole in the ozone layer.

I go out into the garden for a smoke. The heat and smell from the kitchen follow me out, leaving my hair and clothes, dissolving in the crisp outdoors. I light a cigarette, take a long, blessed drag and exhale. Dad's shed is leaning ever-so-slightly to one side. A windowpane winks at me. I try and see in but it's too dark. On the windowsill there are some leggy, barren geraniums in pots. Mother always insists on her green fingers, but her plant-care regime only stretches to chucking water over everything until it's dead. She starts to cough behind me. I know she's glaring through the window. As I turn I see her waving her arms about in the kitchen. She's pushing my smoke back outside. It looks as if she's saying 'go away, be off with you'. Then she lunges forward to bang the window shut. She's washing-up with a vengeance.

I stub out my cigarette and go back in. Mother's face is shining with grease. She's singing a hymn about marching on to that city, and doesn't stop when I take the cloth out of her hand. Stop, Mum, I say, have a rest. She snatches the cloth back, as if it's her soul I grabbed when she wasn't looking. Don't you know the devil makes work for idle hands? she says, and goes back to wiping and singing. As I walk toward the front door she follows me. What's your latest been doing today? she says. His name is Rob, Mum, I say. Hope he's not tiring himself out playing his guitar, she says, as she stands in the doorway polishing a plate. All that strumming, it could give him, what's it called? you know, repetitive strain injury. I aim a peck on her cheek. Bye, I say, thanks for lunch.

In the car I wind the window down and light another cigarette. My mouth feels coated with chicken grease. I feel impregnated with veg fumes. I want to shower, clean my teeth. I take the scenic route home, and smoke three cigarettes, one after the other. My throat begins to feel raw. I pull into a supermarket car park. The store looks like a glass cathedral. Music plays inside. I walk briskly through the vegetable section, averting my eyes. I join the people moving slowly up and down the aisles. Everyone seems peaceful. I buy a ready-made pasta meal for Rob, some garlic bread and a bottle of red wine. Near the checkout they have buckets of red roses. I buy three huge bunches and pay with plastic. Back in the warm car, the roses' perfume intensifies.

As I draw up outside the flat it's in darkness. From the lounge window I see the flickering blue electric glow of the TV. I run up the stairs and open the front door. There's some cookery programme on. The phone rings and I pick it up, dropping the pasta and flowers. It's Mother. She tells me I forgot to take the bag of onions she left by the front door for me. Never mind, I say, next time. I put the phone down with a bang, leave the things where they fell on the floor and go into the lounge. Rob is lying down on the sofa reading one of my magazines. Hi babe, I say, watcha been doing? Nothing much he says, and smiles through a yawn. I fall on top of him and he wraps his arms and legs around me. I take a deep breath of his hair and neck. Mmmm, I could eat you all up, you beautiful couch potato, I say, and kiss him on the mouth.

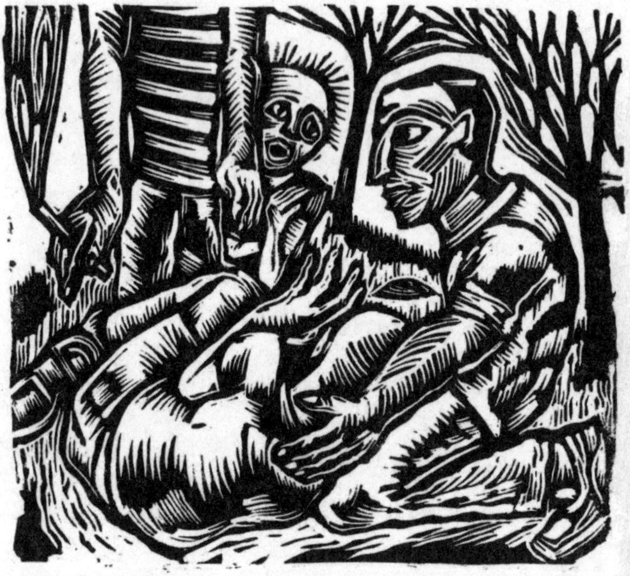

Exile all the Longer

João Morais

It is a nice clear day down the park and in front of me is some old boy playing frisbee with his son. He is shaped like an orange with cocktail sticks for arms and legs. You can tell he got a posh grammar swede cos it don't look like he's ever done much casual labour. And his son is going the same way and all. His hoody clumps to his paunch and you can already see his hips widening.

When it's the son's turn to throw, the old boy can't catch the frisbee. It falls out of his hands again. His muscle memory belongs to a thinner, younger man. And he's clumsy as well, like you would expect his son to be after each growth spurt. But you can tell that no matter how crap and tired he is, the old boy is really enjoying their time together. He smiles between all his puffs and blusters and he's watching the nipper as if he was bringing joy to the world just by standing around and being alive. It's the kind of thing that makes you remember what dads are actually for.

At the same time the old boy jumps half a foot off the ground to try and catch a frisbee that is fifteen feet in the air, I clocks my brother walking through the castle gates. The old boy grabs the top of his belly, or maybe even his lower chest, like he might have given himself a hernia somewhere. But there ain't no time to see his next throw, which probably won't even reach his son again anyway, cos a text comes through.

Ru sat on the rocks? Cant cu

You can always see someone like Gez getting close to you as he's so big, cos he's the one who took after dad. That's the thing with being an endo. You looks at Gez's slim face and it's not the type that looks like it belongs with such a fat arse. If he started deadlifting and pressing twice a week, he could be stronger and bigger than everyone else in about three months. But like the old boy between us and dad before him, he'd rather cover up his slabs with a baggy t-shirt instead of doing anything about it.

Gez spots me and smiles as he walks over. It's one of those sunny days where that deep blue from the sky comes down and jacks everyone up with its happiness. The park is rammed out. Every time some scrote who thinks it's cool to wear a woolly hat on a day like this gets a ball too close, I boots it as hard as I can towards the river. Then I turns to him and offers my arms out wide, asking him and his spars what they're gonna do about it. And all they ever do is bitch and moan and get a little bit more accurate with their kicking. But then when Gez is walking over, the old boy fucks up by missing another catch. So I gets off my arse and walks over to him with the frisbee. He looks like he ain't ever seen another human being before, the way he is looking at me and panting. I passes him the frisbee and he don't even say thanks. But it ain't worth cursing him out cos I wouldn't have moved if I didn't wanna help him. And if there's anyone who should be having fun, it's a little one with their dad.

There ain't no point raising the tension, so I looks around and finishes off my smoke as I waits for Gez. To the left of my feet, a marching line of ants makes their way to and from this abandoned polystyrene box that probably once held a kebab. One or two are struggling to carry these giant crumbs of pitta bread back to HQ. Gez sits down without speaking. I offers him a smoke but he don't take it.

In front of us, the old boy bends slowly to pick up the frisbee. By the way he rocks off the balls of his feet, you can tell he's feeling the rising pressure in his knees. Each second longer it takes him to pick up the frisbee lets him catch his breath a little more. But he has to keep playing on, cos he don't want his son to miss out, and he don't wanna miss out on his son. Maybe he's got some plush number in a big office somewhere and feels guilty for being away from home all the time.

I turns and faces Gez. 'I can't believe it's been another year,' I says.

Two magpies rush past overhead, like they got stuff to

do. They ain't like the people all playing frisbee or football and flapping their gums in the heat like tomorrow don't matter.

The old boy chucks the frisbee too high and too far, and when the son has to run a fair distance to pick it up, the old boy takes the chance to sit down. But by the way he don't take his eyes off his son, you knows he has to carry on. Cos he knows how his son feels, cos he felt the same way once and all. The old boy's son is at that age where you goes around saying 'My Dad's Harder Than Your Dad' and it really matters, because he ain't yet realised that his dada is just another weak human being like anyone else. But one day, he'll know that his dad can fuck things up just as much as the rest of us can.

Gez stops checking out some girl and turns to me. 'Just give me a blydi spliffen so I dun have to think about it,' he says.

I holds out my fist, and he crashes his into mine.

We don't talk while Gez skins up. All we can hear is what's around us. There ain't nothing like the sound of birds tweeting and cars roaring. There ain't nothing better than all that laughter and chatter and then hearing the chimes of some clock striking four, and knowing you got the rest of the day and night still to go. Even the occasional kid falling over and bawling can't dampen anyone's mood.

Gez sparks up his spliff, but there ain't no stink cos we're being licked by a nice cool breeze, and it's even bringing over the smell of burnt meat from some distant barbecue. The old boy in front of us is sat on the floor with his legs spread out. His whole torso is pumping up and down. His son goes up to him but he don't sit. The son just leans over and puts his hand on his old man's shoulder. You gets the feeling that it should be the other way round.

'He would have loved it down here today,' Gez says. 'It's nice and bright and there's room to kick a ball. And we would be old enough now to go for a pint with him after as well.'

I takes the spliff off Gez so I can forget and all. He's watching the bin in front of us. It is so full that there is more rubbish in the plastic bags around it than could ever have fitted inside. The whole busy thing is buzzing with wasps, and they're all desperate to get their munch on. From this distance, it looks like a space port from some film your dad might have put on when you was a nipper.

I'm just about to answer that he couldn't have kicked a ball much longer the way he used to eat and drink when the old boy's son starts shouting. His old man is on the floor behind him, and the son is yelling out to anyone who might listen. The scrotes with the woolly hats stop kicking the ball, but none of them moves. With the noise all around and the number of people, almost everyone keeps on flapping and ignores the nipper.

'Fuck, I'd best go over,' Gez says. 'Only course worth going to was the first aid one they put me on last year.'

He gets off his arse and jogs the forty yards to the old boy, who is spark out on the floor. Gez gives him a prod and then puts his ear to his mouth, then turns and yells my name. Then Gez starts shoving both his palms into his chest like the old boy owes him money.

When I gets off my arse, I notices that the colours of the trees are almost as lush as the sky. It's that time of day. Just before sunset, when the light is at its lowest point, when it is smacking you bang in the swede from the tightest angle, just before it disappears under the horizon. That's when the sun shines the brightest.

I jogs over to join them. The son looks at me and his eyes go from big to normal, like I'm gonna make it all better. 'Don't worry kid,' I says. 'We'll sort him out now, standard.'

The son can't quite bite his lip cos he's breathing in and out so heavy. When he looks around for more help, I takes the chance to speak to Gez. 'This old boy don't look too good, bro.'

Gez stops puffing in his mouth and starts pressing on his chest. 'I knows that, now call a fuckin ambulance, quicktime.'

The old boy's son can't be older than eleven, but already he's got one of those faces that knows how it sees the world. And you don't need to clock his accent to know he's only down for the day, cos he wears his town on his face. He probably just bought the frisbee but couldn't wait to get home to play with his spars, and made his old man play before they got the train back up the Valleys. I makes the call and I asks the nipper his name, and his old man's name. Then I gives him my blower and tells him to call his mumma, but he says she ain't around no more and he asks to call his nana instead.

You can hear the sirens when the ambulance is thirty seconds away, and then it smacks the kid that this is real. The ambulance comes right through the castle gates and about a hundred people has to get out the way when it drives over the grass, and the nipper starts bawling.

You wants to tell him it will be okay. You wants to make a joke of it, telling him what it's like. That the worst part about not knowing who your old man was properly is not knowing how bald you're gonna be one day.

Gez gets in the back of the ambulance after the old boy is stretchered in. When I looks down at the kid, he's somehow holding my hand. He's looking up at me but he ain't saying fuck all. And then I realises. For the first time, I'm the adult here. It don't matter about what I think or feels, it's all about the nipper. And for all you can work out, he might be left with only his nana before long and all.

'Look,' I says. 'I ain't got my mumma around neither, nor my dad. They never wants to leave you. Your old man will pull through, cos he ain't thinkin about himself at the moment, he's thinkin of you in his swede there. Now get in the back of that ambulance and go hold his hand.'

I lifts the nipper up and puts him in the back, then tells the paramedic to shut the door. The ambulance turns round and goes off on one, blinding everyone with the blue lights and deafening everyone with the siren. But after five minutes of it going, the park is back to normal. The scrotes with the woolly hats start playing football again and everyone else gets back to flapping and laughing. But there's one part of the park that will never be the same again.

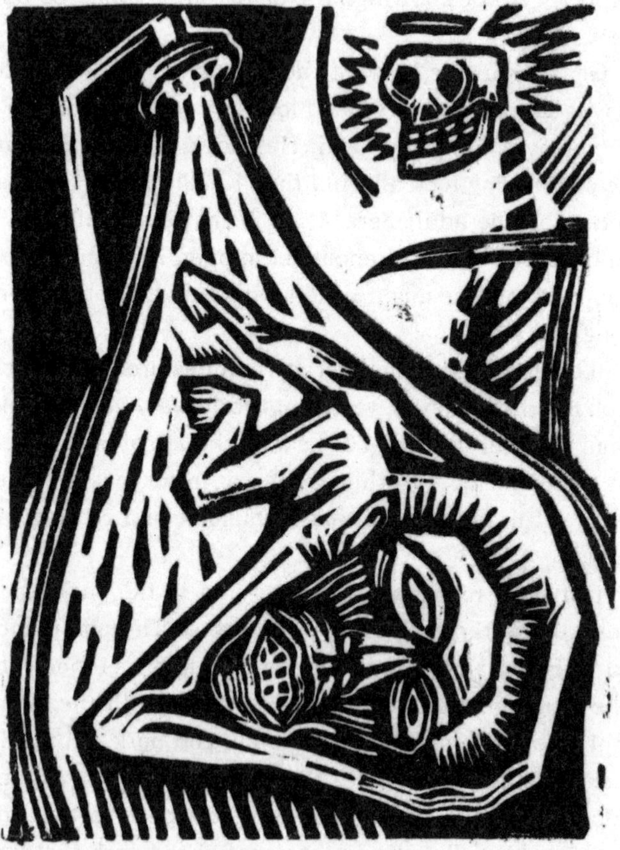

My Cousin's Gun

Holly Müller

Danny had always considered Ben his best cousin. The rest of them were losers, or girls. He thought everyone would understand that he wanted a keepsake to remember him by, so he phoned his sister and asked for the medal. She said she didn't want it anyway, that it just lay in a drawer. She said it made her feel weird – that it didn't seem right chucking it out but it didn't seem right keeping it either. She said it felt like there was death all over her hand whenever she touched it.

Danny called into the cafe to pick it up. The medal was still in the blue paper Ben had wrapped it in, stuffed in her purse.

'Maybe he would've liked me to have it,' Danny says, as she dumps her bag on the freezer lid and rummages for the medal. She's not listening. 'Jackie? Maybe he would've been pleased.'

'Yeah, maybe. I don't really care. I don't want it myself, that's all.'

Danny goes to the park and sits. Ben's funeral is on Thursday. The wrap of blue paper lies in his pocket, a small weight against his thigh. He pauses before taking it out, trying to get into the right frame of mind, trying to feel something – for Ben, for this moment.

Around him the park is hushed. It's five o'clock and the gates will close at six. The air is moist, cloth-like, resting on his skin, chill in his lungs. Plants stand leafless in the flower border beside the bench. Danny tips the medal from its soft blue paper into his palm – highly polished dark gold, star-shaped. At its centre are two crossed sabres. The ribbon is striped, blue, white, red, green – the edge of the fabric crinkled and blackened by fire. The pin is bent into a right angle. The medal is different to how he remembered it – it's smaller, older-looking, alien. There are scribbles across the disc in the centre, beside the sabres. Arabic, he guesses. He'd only caught a glimpse of it on the day Ben gave it to his sister.

'Ripped it off some rag-head,' Ben had said as Jackie unwrapped the gift, everyone watching. Jackie stared at the medal glinting on the dinner table. Ben had always had a thing for her, wanted to impress.

Later that evening after Ben had gone home, Danny sat beside Jackie on the couch.

'Do you realise where it came from?' Jackie said.

Danny had only wanted to see it.

'He shot the person who wore this. Don't you get it?'

He'd only wanted to hold it.

'Grow up, Dan. Don't be a prick. Get off. I'm not letting you touch it. You don't understand.'

Danny was thirteen then. It was just something Ben did, brought trinkets back from Afghanistan, put them on the tablecloth as though they were just ordinary things. Danny didn't question it. It was true that his cousin didn't look how he expected him to, like someone who was fighting in a war. He didn't have a haunted face or nervous twitch or traumatic experiences he couldn't talk about. Instead he lolled in his chair, limbs loose and powerful like a big cat resting in the heat of the day. His blue eyes glowed, with a sheen-like mist just below the surface. He'd always had eyes like that. The army salary was good and trigger time, he said, was a bonus.

He'd flipped Danny's gift across the table.

'Catch.'

Danny fumbled it; the parcel landed with a clatter on his empty dinner plate; his fork, coated in mashed potato, somersaulted onto the carpet. His mum tutted – his cheeks burned.

Once, at Christmas, Ben had snorted Tequila and put salt and lemon in his eye. He could arm-wrestle anyone. He was good at everything. He'd fired a gun.

* * *

He'd let himself into the flat using the spare key – as soon as he'd stepped inside he'd heard water running in the bathroom. Ben had given the key to Danny months before saying he could come round whenever he wanted, if he needed somewhere to hang out, to get away from the parents. Wink, wink. Ben showed him where to find his collection of porn. Danny had coloured up and glanced quickly away from the fascinating images on the magazines and DVDs.

He'd been round to the flat a few times and Ben gave him a beer and they watched a film, not a porno, but an action movie. Ben asked if Danny wanted to make some money and do him a favour, selling weed and pills in town. Danny said yeah, maybe. It felt good that Ben had chosen him.

'You've got a fuck-of-a-lot more sense than most kids your age,' Ben had said.

'Ben. You in there?'

The water hissed. He knocked. Then a second time. He opened the door, just a crack, and called Ben's name. Still nothing. He lingered, took off his coat, flung it over a chair-back. He tried to ignore the faint unease that crept into his belly. He wandered into the living room – the TV was on mute, a takeaway carton spewed unwanted salad onto the coffee table. Danny watched a bit of TV, the sound down low. Twenty minutes passed. He returned to the bathroom door.

'Ben!' he shouted.

He thought, there's nothing wrong, don't be stupid. I'm going to get the piss ripped out of me so badly for this, for freaking out like this.

The first thing Danny saw when he found Ben was the naked expanse of his back. It was red as though it had been whipped and several large bubbles of skin hung, translucent white, trembling beneath the pummelling water. Danny could hardly see him for the steam. It was like standing in the middle of a cloud, like he did once on a school trip to Cumbria, milky vapour pouring over him from the sky. Except this was hot – he was almost choking, his face beaded with sweat. Eventually he leaned across, switched off the shower, and stood back. It didn't seem real at all.

The pathologist said later that Ben must have haemorrhaged about three hours before he was found and died from the brain injury. He'd been punched in the head the previous night while he was queuing at the cash point on the High Street. He'd been knocked out – hit once behind the ear, according to witnesses – but once was enough. He'd got into a ruck in the club where he'd been drinking, had bad-mouthed a guy at the bar for slopping beer down his leg. The guy had followed him out.

Danny had always had a thing about death. He used to dream about it. He'd obsessed over it when he was a small child. He wanted to know about it any chance he got. Perhaps he even wanted it in his life. Death was the real thing. If you didn't know about it, you were out of the loop until you did. And he'd always been one of those kids who didn't know yet, waiting to be knocked down. He used to find himself imagining, wishing that his family would be wiped out, or some of them at least. It would happen suddenly, he'd be torn from what had been and thrown into something bigger – something that would make more sense than his everyday life, where he felt nothing big at all.

When that thought came, he snatched it back as quick as it arrived, in case he jinxed them or sealed their fate. But he always felt exhilarated too for the same reason, in case it was coming, just around the corner.

* * *

Danny gets up from the park bench, needing to move. He hadn't realised he was so cold. He jogs home along the river, along the deserted cycle path. He can see the white flash of his trainers, the light almost gone, the river to his right covered in scribbled reflections from the streetlamps. He cuts through the alleyway that leads to the cul-de-sac, rounds the corner, comes to a halt, breathless. He faces the house – the lights are on downstairs, the red lamp in the lounge glows through the curtain, there's the blue strobe of the TV. His mum and dad will be wondering where he is. He likes letting them worry sometimes; he often pauses before going in, enjoying being outside and them not knowing he's out there, watching.

He leans against the wall and puts his hands in his pockets for warmth, feels the medal, closes his fingers around it.

Ben's dead, he thinks. And I'm alive.

He thinks how easy it is to die. The man who wore the medal is dead. The man who shot him is also dead. Everyone dies. Danny tries to imagine dying, but can't. Not now, not yet – not ever. He tries to imagine killing.

He thinks about Ben, bracing the gun against his shoulder, as familiar to him as his own arm. He imagines an Afghan soldier – maybe he was running, the medal bouncing on his chest. Danny thinks about the heart in the chest of the Afghan, the only one he would ever have. The bullet soared from his cousin's gun.

Danny remembers a moment when Ben was still a kid, when Danny was very small. Ben kicked a ball in Danny's face on the beach at Scarborough, smacked him to the ground with the force of the blow. Uncle Simon, Ben's dad – who was smearing sun lotion over his new girlfriend's back – had reared from his towel like an angry elephant seal. He'd grabbed Ben by the arm and slapped him several times spitting curses then punched him in the side of the head with a vicious downward crash of his fist. Ben had wailed and clutched himself.

Danny realises that his cousin could have died right then instead, before he became a man, before he became a soldier, a killer of other men.

* * *

The cars stand in a black line beyond the wall. The high roof of the hearse shines in the afternoon sun like a pristine engine, the other cars like the carriages of a sombre train. A gentle breeze ruffles Danny's freshly cut hair. The family are waiting outside the crematorium. Another funeral booked in before them is due to finish then it will be their turn. The afternoon is quiet, cars purr on the street beyond – the sky blazes autumnal blue. Danny has a feeling of unreality again. Even while they'd followed the black cars from the Chapel of Rest, he'd felt that something was missing. He'd sat in the back while his parents talked about the utility room carpet, how it could do with a proper clean, because the dog had brought in a lot of mud.

The doors of the crematorium open and the other family appear – they shuffle to an area where flowers are laid on the ground. Some of the flowers are shaped into letters.

'DAD' says one red and white display.

'JOHN' says another.

The coffin is on a raised plinth – behind it is a scarlet curtain. A priest stands at a lectern to the left hand side. The wallpaper is marble-patterned, grey squiggles on white like veins. Danny sits beside his sister, hoikes his trousers.

'We have come here today to remember before God our brother Ben.'

They stand for a hymn – then sit. The priest speaks for a long time – he has a musical voice, like the soft babble of birds. The family respond in chorus to his intonations and cross themselves now and then. Danny's mind drifts while the words of the priest continue in their drowsy rhythm.

A phone buzzes – buzzes again. The man seated directly in front of Danny fumbles in his pocket to silence it. Danny's reverie is broken and he glances around, hoping no one has noticed his daydreaming.

Eventually, the priest has finished and surreptitiously presses a button beside the lectern. The coffin jolts and then glides forward along a conveyor belt. The red curtains part with a loud electric hum – one of Ben's sisters begins to cry. Uncle Simon lifts his chin as though he is trying to balance something there.

Danny had considered bringing the medal with its scorched ribbon and putting it in the coffin beside Ben's body, burning it with him as a gesture of some kind, though he didn't know what it would have meant exactly. Something to do with respect and everyone being equal. But he hadn't in the end – the medal was still in his room, stored in the snap-lid plastic box where he kept significant things.

The foot of the coffin disappears, swallowed by shadow. The curtains close.

Danny pictures the white heart of the fire, the orange glow, the coffin jammed inside a chamber, no space, only heat and fierce burning. How does a whole body fit into a tiny urn? Does some of it get lost? Does some of it fall through a grate or blow out of the chimney? Or was a person really that small, once all the water was gone from them? Danny gets an ache in his throat, which spreads to his mouth. He imagines a pork joint, charred and running with juice. The congregation rises around him so that he's trapped into his pew. He has the urge to vault the back of it and make for the door, for fresh air. He takes a deep breath and his sister puts her hand on top of his and squeezes. Danny looks at her. They stay seated together, waiting.

Perhaps, thinks Danny as the people go out of the door, I'll develop a fear of fire. Or of clouds, like the clouds of steam in Ben's bathroom. Or perhaps not, seeing as nothing else had turned out quite like he imagined. Perhaps, he thinks, I'll never use a gun. And I'll keep the medal to remind me of the Afghan. I'll tell Jackie that I'm older now, and that now I understand.

There's another group of people outside the crematorium waiting to go in, dressed in black and huddled like penguins.

Danny and Jackie follow their family over the tarmac to stand beside the flowers.

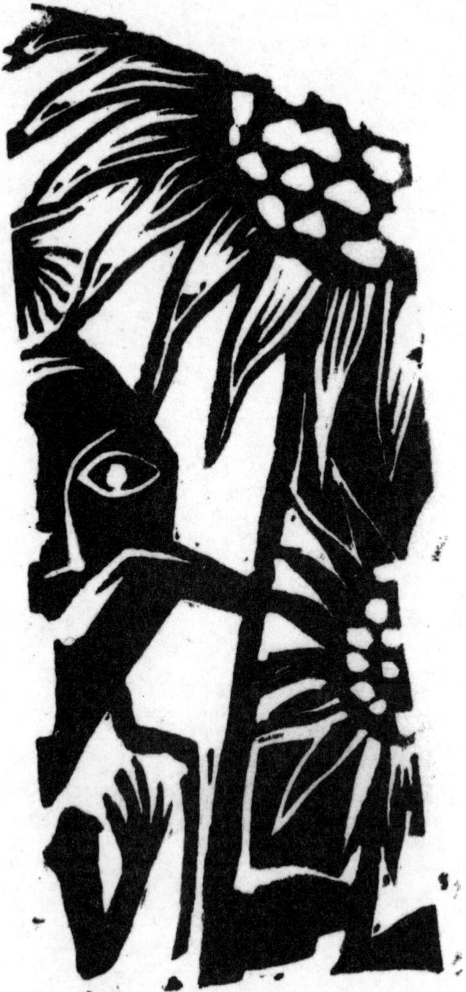

Holiday of a Lifetime

Rachel Trezise

The blackberries are fresh and bittersweet; releasing a sharp kick when I force and burst them against the back of my teeth. Auntie Lynette is back from the market in Narberth, she's left a punnet for my mother on the worktop. 'You want to wash that muck off your face, gul,' she says watching me slyly as I pick at them. 'You've got more eyeliner on than that bloody Winehouse piece.' I look up from my phone, glaring at the clear plastic patch stuck on her fat, mottled shoulder. I decide to leave her comment go. She's trying to give up smoking; she's in a bad mood.

There's a gush of water as my mother fills the kettle. 'Doctor Gwilym says her body just gave up,' she says, talking now about Auntie Marilyn, who was my real auntie. Lynette is only a neighbour. She lives next door, but she may as well live in our house the way she walks in without knocking, banging on about what I am and am not old enough to do. 'Perhaps she died of a broken heart,' my mother continues, flicking the kettle's switch. 'No apparent reason, it just stopped beating.'

'Have you ever heard such claptrap?' says Lynette; so cynical.

I'm flipping back and forth between recent text messages from Osian and Rhodri, wondering which one of them I should take to the funeral. My mother's said I can take a friend for company, but only one. She's a stingy cow and she reckons the buffet isn't big enough for eleven of us. Osian is my first choice, obviously; dark and lanky. I've just had my braces off and I want to kiss him first. I lick at the enamel of my newly freed teeth, imagining it, envisioning him playing his bass guitar at the school concert, the insides of his forearms milk-white and marbled with raised blue veins, his dog tags glinting beneath his shirt collar. But I know in my gut that I should pick Rhodri; ginger and thickset, polite and well behaved.

'It'll be that inbred with his black magic,' Lynette says. 'You know what they're like.' It takes me a few seconds to work out who she's talking about. Marilyn had made friends with one of the gypsy men from the Westover site a few years back. Lynette was adamant they'd been sleeping together, that the gypsy'd been after Marilyn's money. The council has evicted most of them this summer. There are only six caravans left.

'Well, the coroner says there's no explanation,' my mother says. 'They've recorded the death as exhaustion.' Lynette pulls her tobacco inhaler from her handbag and sucks on it. 'Nothing but a bunch of thieves,' she says. 'I'll bet my life it was one of them who got hold of my lighter all those years ago, filched it from the Fishers Arms beer garden. They thought it was worth something, I'll bet.'

The memory comes flooding back like molten lava, my heartbeat a bass drum. I shuffle off the top of the washing machine, the blackberry juice dripping down the insides of my fingers, wine red, like menstrual blood. I sit on the settee in the living room, out of sight. Back then Lynette smoked real cigarettes. She'd clog the kitchen up with her yellowy grey fumes. Sometimes it got so thick I couldn't see my way to the fridge. My mother'd go around with a can of air freshener before my father got back from the Fishers, because he didn't like Lynette coming around, putting ideas about new handbags and shoes into my mother's head. This one time, three years ago, I was sat in exactly the same place, eleven years old, listening to them gossiping. Lynette had started a new ciggy, a hiss of gas from her lighter. I loved Lynette's lighter because it was a pistol, an imitation pistol, with a shiny silver barrel and muzzle, and a pretty mother of pearl handle. She'd bought it from a stall in Blackpool and I wanted to borrow it, to take it to school. But Lynette loved her lighter too; because she was a chain smoker it was never out of her sight. I was pressing my head against the radiator. Sometimes I could trick my mother into thinking I was poorly by doing that. I'd keep it there until the heat was too much to stand, my brain warm and pulpy as if it was about to melt and drip from my ear canals like candle wax. 'Ah, Mammy's little princess,' she'd say, baby-talking, brushing the back of her hand against my forehead.

I heard Lynette going for the ashtray on the windowsill, an oyster shell I'd found on Rhossili Beach. 'I saw her,' she said, talking about my Auntie Marilyn, 'in the Ivy House tea room.'

'Oh yes,' my mother said. 'She likes to take her afternoon tea and scone. She thinks she's the bitch's tits, my big sister.' She said 'bitch's tits' in English, her mouth full of spit, as if swearing in a different language wasn't really swearing at all. I distinctly remember wishing that I had a sister just so that I could call her a bitch.

'But that's not it,' Lynette said. 'She was with someone. A boy is all he was, one of them gypsies from off that Westover site. I hate to tell you, really. It's embarrassing for me.' She loved every syllable in that sentence. Then she lowered her voice and I had to tilt my head towards the doorway to hear her. 'French kissing, tongues and everything. And him unshaven and smelling like the trout he's been stealing out of the Tâf.' She sucked on her ciggy.

'Tongues?' my mother asked.

'Aye, looked like. Cosied up in the snug. Canoodling, like.'

Now another memory washes over me like a wave; the time I got the English words *canoodling* and *canoeing* mixed up. I was on a daytrip to Cenarth with Rhodri and his father when I saw an old feller in a little wooden boat, sailing down the river towards us. 'Look,' I said, pointing. 'There's a man there canoodling.' Rhodri laughed so hard he dropped his ice cream in his lap, the raspberry sauce and sprinkles of hundreds and thousands sticking to his trousers. Gwynfor tutted.

'Technically,' he said spitting on a hanky he'd whipped from his pocket, 'they're coracling. Those boats are called coracles; traditional Welsh fishing boats.'

After Lynette's French kissing revelation, I had trouble trying to imagine Auntie Marilyn with one of the dirty gypsies from the Westover site. It was like Marilyn was chocolate cake and the gypsy was corned beef gravy. You couldn't put them in the same bowl. Besides, I knew that Marilyn still loved Uncle Elvis. Derek had died two years earlier. We called him Elvis because after a few pints he liked to sing 'Are You Lonesome Tonight?' on the karaoke in the Fishers. He had a white silk jumpsuit and glue-on sideburns. Every year he competed in an Elvis competition down south. They played 'Are You Lonesome Tonight?' at his funeral and Auntie Marilyn collapsed, smashing her knees on a marble gravestone. After that we found out he'd gambled their lifesavings away. My mother told me that he'd donated the money to the bookmakers in Llanelli because he liked watching the racehorses going round and round the track. D'uh. Auntie Marilyn moved into my grandparents' bungalow on the edge of the Cwmllan woods. 'She's only staying there temporary,' my mother said. Because really the bungalow was ours, and my mother's a stingy cow.

She wasn't on good terms with Marilyn because of the way Marilyn had acted after my last Nativity Play in the junior school. My mother was excited because I was playing Mary and on the night my voice was loud and clearer than Angelina Carter's from Meadow Croft. Rhodri was Joseph and Osian the innkeeper. When Rhodri and I approached the little cardboard prop inn at the edge of the stage, Osian appeared, his arms folded, his face spiteful. He stared at me, then at Rhodri. 'Mary can come in,' he said, 'but Joseph can eff off.' I wasn't worried but in the car on the way home my mother told me not to worry. 'Osian is jealous,' she said, 'because Rhodri got a bigger part.' Suddenly Marilyn cackled, loud and crazy as a shithouse rat, slapping her legs over and over. 'Ten years old and effing and blinding like a good 'un,' she said.

'What's the matter with you?' my mother hissed at her. 'Our Lleucu practised long and hard for that part. It's not funny. It's a bloody disgrace. That's what comes of divorce, that is. Kids who need their mouths washed out.'

'Oh, you mollycoddle her, gul. There's no harm done.'

'What would you know about it?' my mother spat. 'You never had any kids.' And that was the start of their not talking, which has lasted until now, all because of Osian, wicked, stunning bastard that he is.

On the first day of the summer holidays between junior school and comprehensive, I got up and poured my cereal. I was going in the fridge for the milk when I heard my mother crying in the downstairs bathroom. The door was open; my mother sitting, trousers-up on the toilet, pulling tissue paper from the toilet roll dispenser to wipe at her pink and blotchy face. 'That sister of mine's a liability,' she said, talking to the shaggy blue mat on the floor. 'Merry as the day is long and selfish as a fox.'

'Mam,' I said, to show her that I was there. She looked at me, but with no recognition in her face. She chose a spot on the wall behind my shoulder and started bawling again. 'To think of her rutting around with a teenager, a gyppo no less, and her poor Derek, still warm.' The toilet paper came to an end, the cardboard carcass spinning. I'll have that later, I thought, to make a toilet roll spaceship. 'She's already had her share,' my mother said. 'She had the car and the savings. Oh, she had to spend it, didn't she? On a luxury cruise of all things. "Holiday of a lifetime", she said. Holiday of a flaming lifetime! Well the house is mine. She'll lose it, I swear. They'll trick her they will. It's easy enough. Where's my holiday of a lifetime? Even Lynette goes to Blackpool once a year.'

She hadn't been on holiday since she'd married my father. She still hasn't. It's all she ever goes on about, that and the handbags and the shoes. But I know she doesn't really want to go on holiday because once when my father suggested she go away with Auntie Lynette she said she'd rather do a shift in the fish shop than go to God-awful Blackpool. 'That's not the kind of holiday I'm talking about, Lionel,' she said, snapping at my father. 'I'm talking about Crete, Majorca, the Med somewhere, I don't know.'

'I'm hungry, Mam,' I said, bored and going back to my cereal. When I actually got to open the fridge, that's when I saw it from the corner of my eye: a sunray bouncing off the polished cylinder. Auntie Lynette had left her lighter on the windowsill. It was there – big as tomorrow, sat next to the old oyster shell. I got a foothold in the washing machine door and stretched up, reaching for it. It was light, and simultaneously heavy, a jewel in my little hand. I stroked the pearl inset with two fingertips, the feel of it smooth and hard against my skin. My mother was moving around in the bathroom, the tap running. I slipped the pistol into my gingham dress pocket. Three thoughts came to me, very quickly, one after the other. I couldn't take the gun to school because the school was closed. I couldn't take the gun to Osian's house because Osian had gone to his father's place in Trimsaran. It might have been my only chance to borrow the gun, to show it to somebody, so I decided to take it to Marilyn's on the edge of the Cwmllan woods. And maybe, if the gypsy was there, the gun would scare him away.

To get to Llandewi Velfrey I had to go along West Street and past the Westover Caravan Park where the gypsies had set up camp. They'd been there for five months, their rubbish piling up next to the outer wall. I could see a mattress and a heap of black bags long before I got anywhere near. Later we found out it was the Evans family from St John Street who'd been fly-tipping the rubbish, but back then I was scared of the caravan site, mainly because Auntie Lynette kept telling me that if they caught me the gypsies would steal the gold out of my teeth. I could hear the kids screeching in their funny accents; English with a strange twang that sounded like they had a handful of gravel in their gobs. 'Twt lol,' my mother called it: gobbledygook. They were playing; riding a cob horse saddleless, from one side of the field to the other. I was sad that Osian had gone to Trimsaran, and that we couldn't play cowboys with Lynette's lighter, and that I wasn't allowed to play with him anymore anyway because he was from a broken home, and suddenly I wanted to turn back, but I couldn't, in case Lynette had come around looking for her pistol lighter.

It turned cold when I got off the main road and onto the narrow country lane leading to the house, the tall hedges blocking the sunlight. My shins had turned to gooseflesh and I was thirsty as a goldfish that'd jumped out of its bowl. I remember thinking specifically about a goldfish that'd jumped out of its bowl because the school goldfish had jumped out of its bowl on the last day of term and Rhodri'd had the blame because he was on goldfish duty. I was hoping that Marilyn had Coca-Cola because usually people without kids only had tea or coffee, squash if you were lucky. I got to the stone grit-dispenser and noticed it was shaped like a coffin. It was there so that Marilyn could sprinkle rock salt on the ice in the winter. I knew that, I must have, because I'd been there a few months earlier with my father to deliver the rock salt. But because of what it was shaped like I couldn't help thinking that the gypsy had killed someone and hidden them inside. Osian had been telling me vampire stories. He loved telling me vampire stories. I walked so fast I got a stitch but I didn't stop until I saw the pink shingles of the bungalow through the gaps between the elm trees.

The fishing flies that my grandfather collected had gone from the drainpipe on the veranda where he tacked them, their fuzzy, luminous wings fluttering in the wind, belying the razor-sharp fish hooks hidden inside. A row of drooping sunflowers bordered the house, their leaves twisted and brown. I crept up the steps and onto the veranda, going to the window, my hands shaped into binoculars. The window was smudged with Auntie Marilyn's cat's paw prints. It took a while for my eyes to adjust. Then I saw her, lying on her settee, her long skirt hitched up to her thighs. Her legs were white and lumpy with purple varicose veins. The gypsy was standing up, almost touching the low ceiling, the beginning of a faint black moustache on his upper lip, a waxy fisherman's coat around his shoulders. I must have gasped as he kneeled down adjacent to Marilyn's bare legs. He began to rub something, some ointment into her swollen knees, his hands slow and gentle, Marilyn's eyelids heavy, a half smile on her orange lipstick mouth.

The floorboards on the other side of the veranda creaked. I stepped back, my guts in my mouth. A gypsy boy was slumped on the step in front of the door, his face partially hidden behind the sunflower leaves. He opened his eyes, surprised, and sat up straight, his dark hair clipped to the skull apart from three knotty rat-tails hanging down to his waist, stiffened with grease. His skin was the colour of tea, except for a silver bruise on the inside of his calf, visible through a huge rip in his dirty blue jeans. 'This isn't your house,' I told him, going tentatively for the pistol in my dress pocket.

The gypsy boy smiled at me, dimples in his cheeks like he'd been stabbed with the point of a compass. 'Going to kill me now are, ye?' he said. He talked so quickly it was hard to work out where one word ended and the other began. It was like he was singing a tune; no lyrics, just a tune, his voice undulating. 'There's no gold in my teeth,' I warned him. As I did I noticed the chinks of gold in his calm, brown eyes, like little shards of honeycomb submerged in milk chocolate. He wasn't really a boy; more like sixteen or seventeen years of age, and something about the way he was looking at me made the pistol seem useless. My face was as hot and clammy as if I'd kept it against the radiator for a whole hour. I dropped the lighter into the depths of my pocket. 'What's he doing to my Auntie Marilyn in there?' I asked him.

'Me broddur?' he said. I nodded though I didn't know what he was asking.

'Me broddur's a horse trainer. He's lookin' at err knees. 'Cause 'err knees're gone stiff like an ole Vanner's. He can soothe 'em so, make 'em well again.'

'That's alright then,' I said though I didn't really understand.

'Where're yer friends, now?' he asked me before lifting a plastic bottle of water to his mouth and drinking a lot of it down.

'Haven't got none,' I said. I didn't mean to say it. It jumped out like *canoodling* had with Rhodri and Gwynfor in Cenarth. I toed the scuffed wood of the veranda, conscious of my own bare shins, expecting the question to drift away. But the gypsy was watching me, waiting for an explanation. 'I was Mary,' I said.

The boy nodded. 'You've a triangular face,' he said. 'Leadership qualities. They'll come around alright, the redhead missing yous already.' How did he know that Rhodri was a ginger? 'How do you know he's ginger?' I asked him. He shrugged. He didn't say anything about Osian. Osian didn't miss me I realised and at that moment I hated Osian as much as I'd hated anything in my short life, my solar plexus throbbing with sheer fury. The gypsy boy looked at me, his demeanour mild and patient, the sun catching a silver ring on his middle finger and illuminating his dirty, knuckly fingers. A new feeling obliterated the hate, replacing it with an urgent supernatural need in some chasm between my legs. My fingers started to tremble. I retreated down the steps but hoped that he'd call me back. For some reason I wanted to touch his hair, to smooth my fingertips along the length of the rough, rope-like tendrils. I jumped the last step, showing off, and my feet stung as they hit the ground.

'You're not staying to see yer Aunt?' he said.

'Nah.' The thought of his lovely eyes on my bare, bandy legs stopped me from going back, from turning even to peer at him one last time. There was no spit in my mouth, my tongue swollen and cracked. I ran to the main road, my legs numb, the soles of my feet burning with each new step. I stopped at the Penlan stream and took a gulp of the cold, fishy-tasting water. I hid Lynette's cigarette lighter under a mossy rock. Closer to home I rubbed a few splodges of mud on my legs so that I could tell my mother I'd been playing rounders on the rugby pitch. But by the time I got to the kitchen, and to Lynette lighting a cigarette off the ring of the gas cooker, I was a different person; too old to play rounders. I went straight to the downstairs bathroom to wash the mud off my legs.

* * *

Rhodri came to the funeral, wearing a sky-blue suit that Gwynfor'd bought him for last year's football gala. It didn't go with his ginger hair and my mother wasn't pleased, I could tell by her soured face. But she pinned the same Calla Lily buttonhole that our family wore to his lapel, thanking him grudgingly for coming. It could have been worse. It could have been Osian with his luscious new eyebrow piercing. At the reception at the clubhouse, a small group of gypsies form Westover turned up in jogging bottoms and trainers, Lynette staring daggers at them as they lurched to an empty table at the back. I yearned to eyeball the boy I'd met on Marilyn's veranda. I wanted to see his tea-coloured skin, his scraggy dreadlocks. I wanted him to see my straight grown-up teeth, my spray-tanned legs; the way my cleavage bunched in a push-up bra. He wasn't there. He must have belonged to one of the families the council had moved on. The gypsies didn't speak to us. We didn't speak to them. They were first in the queue when the buffet was announced, Rhodri and I at the back. 'Thieves,' Lynette said, fizzing with indignation as she crept up behind us. She glowered at them as they loaded their paper plates with cold pizza.

I wanted to disagree with her but she was still fuming about her simulation pearl pistol lighter. It was too soon to admit I'd taken it without her doing her nut. She was in a bad mood and the news might start her smoking again. I turned to study the gypsies, looking for a redeeming feature I could use in my argument. A dark-skinned, snaggle-toothed boy of eight was cramming handfuls of prawn vol-au-vents into the pockets of his frayed tracksuit.

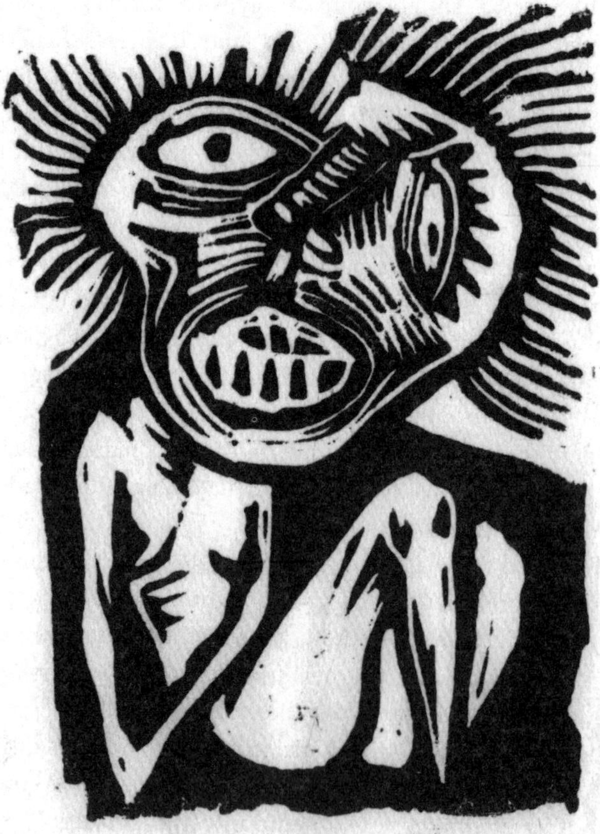

Mangleface

Tyler Keevil

She had been beautiful once. I could tell by the way she walked: straight-backed, long strides, confident. She walked like a beautiful person. The first time I saw her I was putting rentals back on the shelves. I noticed her studying our foreign-film section. I couldn't see her face but I had a good view of her body. That was enough to make me put down my armload of movies and saunter over.

'Can I give you a hand with anything?' She turned towards me. She had her hair styled so that it partially obscured her features, but it didn't really hide much.

'Yeah, I'm looking for–'

She saw my expression. I couldn't help it. The skin of her face was cross-hatched with scars, dry and leathery. Her nose seemed to melt into her lip, which twisted down on one side.

'Never mind,' she said.

I stood beside her for a minute, not knowing what to say, and slunk back to my till in a daze. As she moved around the store I watched her out of the corner of my eye, like I usually did with potential shoplifters. I wasn't satisfied with how I'd left things. After several minutes I tried again.

'Hey, I'm sorry about that.'

She picked up a display box, avoiding my gaze.

'Don't worry about it.'

'You like foreign films?'

A shrug. 'I'm getting bored of the normal stuff.'

I figured if I was in her place I'd watch a lot of films, too.

'That one's all right.' I tapped the case in her hand. It was a film about a film crew following a serial killer around for a documentary. 'Violent, but pretty hilarious. I dug it.'

She smiled at me. It was hideous enough to shatter all the mirrors in the world.

'Thanks,' she said.

* * *

I wouldn't say she came in frequently after that, but she came in regularly. She stopped by in the mornings, when I was the only cashier and the store was empty. On Fridays, she always rented two or three movies. She never came in on weekends.

She walked in one day when I was training a new kid on the till. He served her politely – giving her our usual sales spiel – but after she left he turned to me and asked, 'Did you see good old mangleface there?'

I told him to shut his mouth.

'Sorry,' he said, 'I didn't know you had a thing for her.'

She probably got that kind of comment a lot, from arseholes like him. At the end of the week, I told my manager I'd seen the kid taking pop and pretzels from the confectionary without paying for it, which was something I usually did. He was still on his two-week trial period. That was enough to ensure he didn't get the job.

The nickname stuck, though. I started thinking of her as Mangleface. I never learned her real name. She rented movies on her father's account. I only knew that her last name was Rice. Mangleface Rice. It seemed to fit.

* * *

Mangleface had a boyfriend. I only saw them together once. Once was enough. They made the mistake of coming in just after five. The pre-dinner rush is our busiest time of day. I didn't notice them until they got in the checkout line, which snaked halfway to the back of the store. Between customers I kept an eye on them as they waited. He was dressed in black jeans and a silk shirt – a real cold lampiño. They stood a little apart, muttering to each other occasionally. Everybody was staring, of course, while pretending not to. It was almost like they were celebrities of some sort.

When they reached my till, the guy asked, 'Is this flick any good?'

He thrust the tape into my hands. I glanced at the title on the spine. It was an Italian film about a weird guy driving around on his scooter, looking for Jennifer Biels.

'Sure, it's kind of all right.'

'Kind of all right,' he said to her. 'You hear that?'

'I want it,' she said.

He lowered his head and shrugged his shoulders, then slapped ten bucks down on the counter. I took it and asked him if they wanted any popcorn or candy. I didn't address her, or look at her much, because we were both pretending not to know each other, in that way you do.

'Why would we?' he said.

'I have to ask.'

'We don't want any of that crap.'

I scanned the movie, fed the tenner into my till, and gave him his change. The store had gone quiet. He took the movie and walked out without waiting for her. As she left she glanced at me. It was hard to read her expression, because her face didn't work like a normal face. It always looked sad, clownish, the mouth drooping down on one side as if she'd had a stroke. But there was something resigned about it, as if she knew what was coming, and soon.

* * *

The more accustomed I grew to her disfigurement, the more I was able to ignore it. If there was anybody else in the store, she was anxious, shy. When we were alone, though, she wasn't afraid to talk to me. I learned that she liked pecan ice cream and skiing. Her favourite movie was *Night of the Living Dead* – the original black and white version.

I never asked about her face.

Sometimes, though, when she wasn't looking, I'd check her out. If her back was turned to you she was hot. She had a great body: tanned and lithe and toned. Then you'd see her face, and that would be it. It was pretty unsettling. I wondered if her boyfriend felt similarly. Did they ever have sex? Maybe every so often – but only with the lights out. In the dark it could be anybody's face. He wouldn't kiss her. He'd just grab her tits and squeeze her ass and imagine she was somebody else. That arsehole didn't deserve her. He really didn't.

* * *

I grew used to seeing Mangleface. I looked forward to those morning chats with her. She would linger at my till, telling me what she thought of the movies I'd suggested. I started keeping a copy of the new releases behind the counter, which we weren't supposed to do, in case she wanted to rent one. Sometimes she did, other times she didn't. But the choice was always there.

If she didn't turn up, I got worried. What had happened to her? Maybe she'd had a fight with her boyfriend. I'd wait for her to come running to me. She would be in tears. She would need a shoulder to cry on. Who else could she turn to? Me, of course. I was the only one who could see past the horror of her face.

Other times I imagined she was in trouble. She would rush in, distraught. Somebody was after her. She was sick, injured. She had an enormous debt. Or maybe it was something simpler, like her car had broken down.

Whatever the scenario, I would help her. I'd take care of her.

I had a lot of time on my hands at that video store.

* * *

I was talking to her one day when this guy came in. He wore a pinstripe suit with burgundy leather shoes, and his hair had been lathered with gel. He looked like the kind of guy who managed a bunch of other people for a living. He was drunk, too. Vodka. I could smell it. Drunks think you can't smell vodka, but you can.

Mangleface was at my till. When he saw her he did a double-take.

'Holy shit – what happened to your face!'

Silence. Nobody else was in the store.

'I'm sorry – I don't mean to pry – but Jesus Christ.'

He turned to me. He wasn't trying to be cruel. He was just another arsehole.

'You seen this poor girl's face?'

'I seen it, man. Settle down.'

'I'm sorry. I just couldn't help it. What happened?'

Mangleface had a hard time controlling herself. She was looking down at the movie I'd just handed her. She didn't cry. I never saw her cry, not even once. I sometimes thought her tear ducts might have been damaged, somehow. But her eyes were fine – like she could see all right – so I don't know if that makes any sense.

'Car accident,' she whispered.

'Jesus. That's tough.'

I gave Mangleface her change. She left without saying anything. Even after she was gone he couldn't let it go. He went to window to peer after her. He was really unsettled by it all.

'Did you see that, man? I never seen anything like it.'

He kept saying that. I kept telling him I'd seen it. Eventually he left. Afterwards, I opened up his account and ran a pre-authorization on his credit card for three hundred bucks. We did that for renting games consoles, occasionally. It wouldn't take the money out, but it would freeze the funds indefinitely, until he caught on. It wasn't much, but it was all I could think to do for her.

* * *

I started thinking of Mangleface outside of work. It was weird. My friends and I would be shooting hoops, or down at the beach, and she would be there, in my head. It worried me because that usually only happens with girls I like. Somehow, without my realizing it, Mangleface had become one of those girls. That was okay, I told myself. Nobody has to know. You've got a secret crush on Mangleface – so what? It's not like you're going to do anything about it.

A date with Mangleface would be agonizing. Everybody would stop and stare and wonder what the hell you were doing with a chick whose face looked like that. And those were just strangers. What would happen if my friends found out? I'd never hear the end of it. My friends could be merciless like that.

Some days I wished everybody were blind.

* * *

At night, I began to think of doing things with her. I focused on her body. That was safe. Her body was beautiful. I wouldn't admit to myself what I really wanted. Her body eased me into it.

I imagined running my hands over that body. I was always very tender with her. She was timid. It had been a long time since she'd been appreciated. I took my time, kissing her legs, her belly, her breasts. I didn't look at her face, not at first. I approached it indirectly. I kissed her throat, her earlobes, the nape of her neck.

A few weeks went by before I imagined kissing her face.

It was a frightening experience. Her lips were dry. All the skin on her face was withered like a scorched prune. But I liked kissing her. It drove me crazy kissing those twisted lips. Soon enough we were making love.

I fantasised about that every night for months.

* * *

Though in my head we had gone all the way, during the day our relationship remained chaste. She would come in, wander for a bit, then ask my advice on picking a film. I'd walk with her down the aisles. Sometimes she wanted a horror flick, sometimes a love story. With Mangleface it was never the same. I would take my time helping her. I knew that she appreciated the company as much as my advice. She liked hearing me summarise the plots of films.

'What about this one? It's awesome. There's this guy

who goes around killing people with his electric guitar.'

'His guitar?'

'Yeah. It's got a drill attached to the end. Whenever he hits the strings the drill starts spinning, and he drills people.'

'That sounds hilarious.'

'It is. You'd love it.'

We had pretty similar taste in films. That was part of why we got on so well. Any movie I liked she usually liked. Or maybe she was just being nice to me because I was being nice to her. Maybe she secretly hated all those movies but kept renting them just so she wouldn't hurt my feelings.

I'd never thought of that.

* * *

I knew it was finished between her and her boyfriend when he came in with another girl. She was beautiful. They were both high. In the kids section, I saw him snort something off the back of his knuckle, like a total Carlito. As they stumbled about the store he kept slipping his hand up her skirt. Whenever he did this, she giggled and swatted it away.

They grabbed the latest blockbuster – this movie about an asteroid hitting earth – and came to my till.

'You got your membership card?' I asked.

'I forgot it. I can give you my phone number.'

'Can't rent to you without a card. It's policy.'

I rent to tonnes of people without a card. Not him, though.

'I've done it before,' he said.

'It's a new policy.'

She leaned over the counter so I could see her cleavage, and put her hand on my wrist. 'Can't you make an exception, just this once?' she said, making a pouty-face. 'Just for me?'

I wondered if Mangleface had been like that, before the accident.

'Sorry,' I said. 'I can hold the film for you, if you want to come back.'

'Forget it,' he said. 'Come on – let's go someplace else.'

'Have a good night.'

'Fuck you, pal.'

He flipped me the finger on the way out.

In the parking lot, car doors slammed. An engine roared to life. I looked out the window in time to see his Jetta fishtailing around the corner, the engine whining, the wheels screaming.

I thought for a few minutes, and then went to get three pornos from our adult section. It's a family store but we have this backroom. I got real dirty ones – the dirtiest. I scanned the tapes onto his account, and threw them in our dumpster outside.

I just hoped I was on shift the next time he came in.

* * *

I was happy about the break-up. My fantasies were bleeding into reality. I assumed Mangleface would need me more than ever now that that arsehole was out of the way.

I was surprised when she didn't show up that week, or the week after.

I started to worry. What if being dumped had made her do something crazy? What if she'd killed herself? It had to be something like that. Poor Mangleface. I ran through countless scenarios in my head. She had slit her wrists. She had hung herself. She had overdosed on sleeping pills. She had thrown herself off a bridge. Mangleface was no more. Ashes to ashes, dust to dust.

Nobody would think to invite me to the funeral.

* * *

She came back.

I hadn't seen her for a month. I heard the chime over the door and turned, and there she was. She looked terrible. She'd really let herself go to pieces. She was wearing sweatpants and a dirty shirt and her hair looked like she'd stuck it in a fan.

I pretended not to notice.

'Hey – haven't seen you for awhile.'

Her mouth melted into a smile.

'No,' she said.

'Are you okay?'

'No.'

Then she started sobbing. I had imagined this. I went around to the other side of the counter and held her. She smelled of sweat and felt fragile as a frightened bird in my arms.

'It's okay,' I said. 'It's okay.'

It was just what I'd wanted. I was her great protector.

After a few minutes she stopped sobbing. I held on until it passed, rubbing her back, then let go of her. She still hadn't really cried at all. When she spoke she stared at a point on my chest.

'You know what's strange? I've gotten so used to seeing this face in the mirror that I can't tell how hideous it is anymore. I only remember when I see other people's reactions to it.'

'It's not that bad.'

She sniffed. 'You don't react to it like other people.'

'It doesn't bother me.'

She looked up at me. She had beautiful eyes. They hadn't been damaged at all. They were clear, and blue, and wide open. A baby's eyes.

'But would you ever be able to kiss it?'

I thought of countless lonely nights, of all the times I'd kissed her in my mind, but for a few seconds I couldn't bring myself to act.

That hesitation ruined everything.

The chime above the door rang out like an alarm. Two teenage guys carrying backpacks sauntered in, laughing and shoving each other. That all stopped as soon as they noticed her. One of them whispered something. They stood nearby and pretended not to stare.

Her question still hung unanswered between us.

'I don't know,' I muttered, stepping back.

I barely whispered the words, but she flinched as if I'd shouted. She didn't say anything else. She just turned and walked out. The door swung shut behind her. I stared at the spot where she'd been, as if I could pause or rewind, and play the whole scene again. Get it right, this time.

Those two kids were still standing there, gawking.

'Get the hell out of here.'

They looked at each other uncertainly. One of them tried a smile, as if he thought I might be joking. I wasn't. I started towards them.

'I said get the hell out of here!'

They did. I followed them to the door and slammed it behind them and flipped the lock. Further down the street I could see her, walking away, getting smaller. I leaned against the cold glass and watched her go, feeling like I'd crushed a butterfly in my fist.

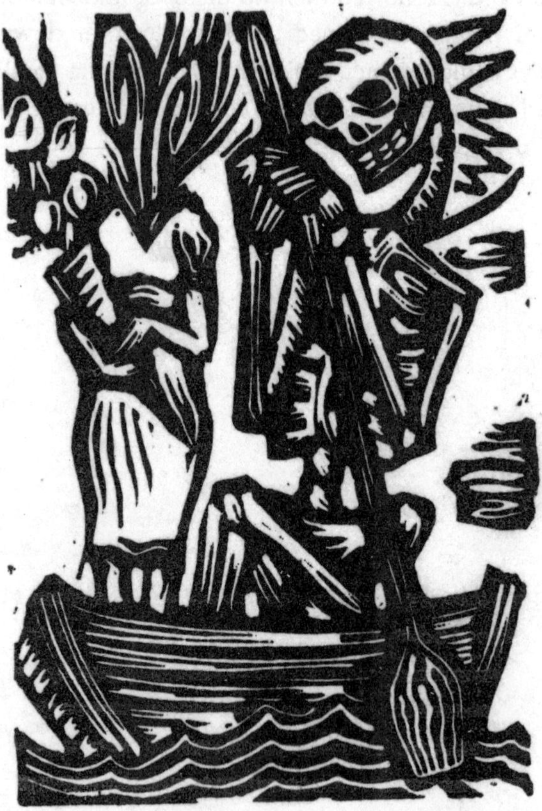

The Bereaved

Georgia Carys Williams

For a time, I resembled the coffee mug on the windowsill: mendable, but with cracks so sporadic, it was difficult to predict when I would next shatter. When it finally happened, it was with all the silence of the first time. My wife witnessed the blood-encrusted vomit on my face and screamed. If I was the mug, she would have picked me up and thrown me once more; my cracked pattern jigsawing at the prospect. Then she would have taken the glue from her pocket and pieced me back together again.

These days, she is awake during the lifeless time of night, when the air is thick with sleeping people. She tries to close her eyes against the dark, but the lengthy echo of silence is what causes her body to sweat; rotates it in eternal frustration, then strands her in the centre of this dire, domestic island.

There were visitors once. Flowers were left on the

doorstep as a show of respect. Our home, just one of a terrace, is marked by the crisped cadavers of carnations in the porch; they have broken away into bleats of deep red upon the concrete tiles. Cakes have been left to turn stale in their boxes.

The mood inside is similar to that of a bleak bed and breakfast. There are too many dull guests gorging on grief. They are dark, lanky beings, drifting like crane flies up the walls, then falling again; their ribs racked under bare-skinned backs and the heads of tenterhook necks attempting to climb and fall, climb and fall. There is a distant look in each eye as their heads lurch to the side. Wherever grief is, they reside, occupying the empty space until the house is heaving with sorrow. Daylight whispers at the windows, but it is a stranger to us all.

One resident, after slumping to the floor, takes a moment to reorient, becoming a limp obstruction in the hallway. I tiptoe over his upturned body and cross the threshold, breaking into what feels like a bell jar of time. The smell of moth-balls tries to cling with dust to my nostrils. Something is sedate; everything, as my feet disrupt nothing but the leanings of the carpet pile. The rest of the residents are still climbing, picking at cobwebs and dropping them like lace onto my shoulders. I try to remove them, but they are entwined in a way that brandishes me in a grey veil.

In the living room, I meet two armchairs sunken at the shoulders from the weight of dog-eared boxes of my belongings. They aren't packed to go anywhere. Instead, there are shirts with the shoulders still shaping them, draped all over the furniture like broken people and as I look around, I see that some of the residents are wearing my shoes.

Everything here once looked after, has been simultaneously abandoned. The dust-tongued rug is hunched up and unwagging, but lies beneath a mossy fish tank; the corpse of one fish trailing from the mouth of the other. I move towards the kitchen, following the rest of the wilted petals but as I step onto the tiled floor, the phone rings and a man's voice interrupts. I look to the hallway, but the words don't follow my ears.

'I'm afraid we're not here at the moment...' says the voice, in a pitch I recognise. 'If you would like to leave a message...' Then it stutters a little. How could I have forgotten it so soon? A resident sitting at the kitchen table turns sharply towards me, then continues to nudge crumbs around the surface. The voice ceases to speak.

This room is in an equally slovenly state; it stores little food but only engraves the obese rings of the unclean oven hobs and a sink mounted with moulded plates, flies glued to solidified food. Mice are eating what could have been the ingredients of something substantial and the kettle stands wrapped up in its own wire. I remember its distinctive whine, its fast whistle over that voice. Then there is a bleep, slow like that of someone flat lining.

The voice has instead transformed to a lady's voice; crackling between careful pauses.

'Dear, I'm worried about you,' it says, 'I know it's been very difficult but...' Then I hear something different; a drone above me. The resident at the table is wrestling the bread crumbs with her fingertips; trying to push them together like Play-Doh. The hum turns into a wail. There is the slow applause of a clock on the wall as I leave the room to ascend the stairs and visit my wife.

The landing seems further away than before as I climb its back, each step a hurdle of socks and underwear as I impose on raw memory. I look behind me to the resident in the hallway: his grey body is twitching as he tries to sit up, but his eyelids are flickering as though they are still asleep through a dreadful dream. The arms of two others appear in a tug around my waist as I try to climb faster, but they eventually let go and I see a familiar belt slouched across the top step.

I hear the muffled wail through a door ajar enough for me to slip through, which uncurls to a loud howl as I enter the misery of magnolia. There is the bereaved, crouched helplessly upon an unravelling patchwork of my life, amongst a mound of my clothes; my dressing gown draped around her clothes-hanger shoulders. Her face is crumpled with pain but clearly tired from its perpetual foldings.

Even though she howls, the air remains still; a congregation of emptiness. I move closer to disrupt it, but as usual, my figure feels no gravity. As I join my wife at knee level, she wrenches the rope of my dressing gown tighter around her middle; the towelling spitting dust and my old aroma in my face. In the muskiness, paper begins to stick to my knees and as I begin to use my voice, I think at first she is stopping me with one hand until the other reaches out; both of them in a hollow embrace. I begin to wonder if she can feel my presence but looking at her face so pale and bloodless, I can't even decipher whether her mouth is open or closed until I hear her sobs again. There are photographs of us mislaid around the room. I peel one away from my knee and smile just like I used to when I felt her hand in the same place.

Then the sobs stop. My wife is searching for something. I begin to doubt she will find it amongst the medley, as her hands trace each item, searching for a particular piece. I feel the urge to touch the underneath of her wrist where it tickles, but she is crying so much that it quivers out of my reach, continuing to search the carpet, just as she had when frantically picking up the pills as though they were the beads of a broken necklace. It finally stops upon my knee, lingers; I remember now: home in the shape of this woman's hand, but it moves again. She has found what she was looking for; a piece of paper folded up so small that it barely exists, like the pills, so small but altogether, deadly. She holds it as though it might leave. There weren't enough pills left to make a necklace. This place is hardly recognisable with so many gathered fragments of me: odd gloves, a hat I rarely wore; old cigarettes and aftershave are dotted around the cluttered floor and soaking up every cavity. The wardrobe doors are open and my clothes have slipped in a landslide onto the carpet; shirts we used to argue over the ironing of are bent at the elbows in a heap of my old identities and trousers lie like the murder marks of dead men around the room. The blinds are shut and the curtains are drawn; hair-clipped together so the light in the room remains dim. I can just about see the mundane mosaic of my coffee mug scattered over the windowsill. My calendar still hangs on the wall, left open at January. It's now July.

The resident from the kitchen has followed me up and is sliding photographs of my face around with her stockinged toes. Around her smooth heels are my old magazines and newspapers piled high. The residents are taking hold.

As my wife hoists her body up, I see that a mousy down has been allowed to creep over her calves; it's cold and erect; a bark of miserable pencil shavings. Oblivious to my visit, she stretches her arms above her head, fingers cobwebbed together. The dressing gown's tie loosens again, shedding from her body and falling to her bony ankles.

Released with a hoarded musk is the body of my young wife; age climbing the walls around her like stubborn fungi. She's beautiful, but I don't attempt to touch her narrowing outline as it gazes through me to the sight of something else – her hair grasping the hollow bulb of her face – then drops straight to the floor with a whimper. For a moment, she'd forgotten.

Above the navy of my dressing gown is a crouched body, her greased hair its only covering. She embraces the gown with a fierce look in her eyes and as always, it yields to her weakness, her body sinking as one does at a graveside; tail-bone dipping into the dust. Her shoulders are so hunched together from whimpering that the blades of her back look like they might never straighten again; her body has control over nothing but the piece of paper in her right fist. As she opens it, I see her lips miming:

Sorry and *forgive me* and *thank you* and *I wish* and *love* and *death* and *escape* and *pain* and *trapped* and *sorry* and *forgive me* and *I wish*

I feel myself crumbling as each word seems to twist something in my stomach, beginning like the sting of cramp but growing to a sickening pain that turns everything into more of a blur as she continues and I whisper alongside.

Love and *death* and *hurts* and *friends* and *family* and *love* and *pain* and
alone, alone, alone,
               forgive me

I look at her again but her head is still bent. From her vacancy, I know the words she has read sound as empty as those engraved on a sympathy card; her neck stiff; eyes still.

'Forgive me,' I try to utter, but my lips only mime too. The bereaved looks towards my face with an expression I've seen once before: there had been vomit acryliced to my skin and a clique of pills around my feet. I was heaped in a corner, head against the bookcase and my knees beneath my chin. She'd retched at the sight of me. I remember my eyes seeing something differently. Then she touched me and screamed.

She is screaming again

and the air has begun to pulsate in sync. with the sound. I feel as though I could topple, but my toes clench the carpet. Before I take another step, a swell of grey glissades past me. All the residents have followed me upstairs and are beginning to swarm around us, their legs clumsily crossing over each other and fighting for space. My wife is shaking as though she can feel their presence, but I've been visited by the residents before, when I was curled up in a ball, trying to unwrap myself from unexplainable sadness. Waking up every day at noon, the world appeared very slightly out of focus, I cradled a heavy burden, which sent my life rotting into the ether. Sometimes, it was interrupted by a flurry of cries. It was then that I began to see the grey figures; I tried to blink them away but they kept calling.

Looking closely at the unearthly residents, I know the droll habits of each one. My wife's uninterested. Her face looks up, but straight through me to the calendar on the wall; days are blacked out like decayed teeth. The paper in her hands however, is an unperturbed white. She reads the words for a second time and I think back to my cries from this very room when there was still a single strobe of light to look at through the v-shape gap in the top of the curtains, until darkness returned so regularly, so unpredictably, and I only dreaded its visits.

The residents are definitely taking hold. They are doubling and tripling around us, closing in and rotating like a circle of ring a-roses where both of us are in the centre, already down. They're pushing against us and tightening around us like a boa constrictor; we are face to face, my wife's breath moist upon my neck. She begins to whimper once more, yanking the dressing gown tighter around her as she does. As dawn creeps further into the room, I see through the curtains to the world I've stepped out of; too large for my wife to step out into without practise.

'I can't forget,' she says again, knowing that no one can hear, her head still and her eyes sinking together. My face feels as rotten as the day she found me; as vacant and detached, as a spider creeps across it. My wife's eyes, with the slant of their brows questioning *why?* But I don't respond; why does anything ever happen? She seems to search my face and sickness tugs at my stomach. This house aches from the core for something to fill it. 'You actually did it,' she says, loudly and clearly. 'You actually...'

The residents have dissipated and are climbing the walls again, but my wife and I remain intimate, her head almost bowed upon my shoulder. If she could hear me, I'd explain how much I didn't *want* to do it. It felt like the only answer for so much pain. I'm crouching over her now as she curls up, begging for a different reality. My letter is once again lost amongst the quarry of me and eventually, her irises freeze; her body resists; any strength she had has dissolved into my lap. We're in the same place for perhaps the very first time.

'It's everything you can't see,' I finally whisper, thinking of the hectic house around her, as she twists and turns again like a doll in my bare hands. She cries into her knees, rocks back and forth, encasing her legs, then drops onto her side, wailing. 'Why?' she cries with her head in her hands and I know the pulling and yearning she feels in her stomach.

I look out the window and see the fickle Welsh weather; sun breaking through the clouds, then giving up. I sense the brush of another spider crossing my face but I still don't move it, allowing it to curtain my hair with its spun thread. The arms of my wife reach out but I stay back until she collapses again, rolling onto her spine with a helpless whimper. The residents are dropping from the walls and landing in piles upon the carpet before they stand, then start climbing all over again.

Breaking the whimper is a voice bellowing through the floorboards; it's the slow murmur of my answer-phone stuttering, followed by the sustained bleep and the same lady's voice speaking.

'Hello again, it's me, love,' but the sound of a little voice from the background breaks to the forefront, transforming into the cry of a child. *Life goes on,* people say. *Life goes on.*

'He's asking for you,' is what I make of the lady's voice, loudening through the ceiling; my mother-in-law. "He's wondering where you are," she adds, but before I clutch onto any more words, the wailing begins again. My wife has shifted back into focus; a weak heap of bony woe. She drains the remains of an exhausted sob; as though she's realising how quickly time is passing even as she collects her breath. She tries to stand, but the resident from the kitchen presses her down at the shoulders. Three faces look up at me from a photo at my wife's weak ankles; for one of them, I hear our son's cries. *Ma-ma ma-ma,* then nothing.

My wife composes herself and at first only rocks like a roly-poly toy before launching her body through the resident's grey arms and finding a stance that doesn't topple. She stares directly at each resident around us, as though acquainting herself with each lost face. If they weren't so limp, she'd shake their hands; finally acknowledging the feeling.

She walks carefully out of the room, carrying nothing but my dull dressing gown; the dust spits at her feet but her breath is the only sound I hear. It's here that I notice the expression of the residents changing for the first time, the void in their eyes filled with longing. Nevertheless, my wife walks towards the bathroom and I follow her in; watch her beginning to shower; observe as she crouches upon the porcelain floor of the bath and feels the warm waterfall upon her grieving, goose-bumped skin.

I imagine I can feel it upon me too; our aches simultaneously disappearing, deep, worn-out muscles numbing under the boil. This is the longest time she hasn't cried for. Her eyes are closed and her frayed mouth is open. She buries her flat chest away from me, beneath wet arms crossed in front of her knees and she lies down at the base; water still beating upon her.

When she eventually steps out of the bathroom, she's dressed in her own clothes, much baggier than before. On the landing, the residents face her in a queue. My wife looks less surprised walking past them, almost lost among the line of grey faces. They've been waiting. They're adorned in my shirts and trousers; walking versions of the broken men in our bedroom. With free rein, they seem to walk in more of a stride and they no longer bother to climb the walls. They're standing in my shoes; toes pressed right to the tips of the leather, more comfortable than I ever made them feel.

Soon, she clears a path downstairs and begins to tidy the mess in the kitchen; closing cupboard doors and scraping food into the bin. Every now and then, she sits in the living room, upon the tired armchair with her head in her hands and she moans at the injustice. As I blink, I see the house emptying around us.

The residents follow my wife into every room; this time the kitchen. They're picking up saucepans and with no ingredients to use, placing every utensil back in the same place. She's making cups of tea and setting them around the house as though for each resident. She feels them dithering around her but she continues to tidy up; their presence as ignored as wallpaper. She's increasingly tolerant of these thieves as the days go on, each evening black-mailed grey and stumbling into the next.

Then she clears up the crumbs, places pots in the sink, dusts the shelves in the living room and undrapes the armchairs. This house is gradually resembling the place we forged together; argued and laughed in; where we brought a blend of us both home in a baby's shawl. *I'm so sorry.*

As grief subsides, the residents are itching to leave; starved of their surroundings; their bored bodies twitch like the one in the hallway. The clock has clapped so many times that its hands must ache and new dust is beginning to settle on the carpet.

I watch to see if my wife will glue my mug back together one more time, but she's only rearranged it upon the kitchen table. She sits for a while, staring at each piece and I wonder what she's waiting for. *Forgive me,* I say, *forgive me*. The doorbell has begun to ring, but she doesn't budge at the sound; her eyes are open, but ignorant. Then it rings again; a long drill of a bell, so constant that she has to stand up.

Eventually, I see her traipsing towards the door. She opens it to visitors; my mother-in-law, who carries a large container of food in one hand, with her grandson clutching onto the other. He releases his grip and gallops throughout the house, exploring every space, panting and gibbering as though silence was never here. My mother-in-law stands in the porch, smiling, then strides through and throws open the curtains of every downstairs window.

My wife's not ready for this, I think, feeling daylight harsh upon my face. Then I hear her voice from another room.

'You mustn't touch that,'

but it's too late; having followed her back into the kitchen, I see that our son has headed straight for what must have appeared to be a colourful jigsaw. Before there is a chance to stop him, he picks up one of the pieces, then quickly drops it again, recoiling at the sharpness of its edges upon his tiny fingers. The shock, like being bitten, has filled his eyes with tears; his bottom lip protruding as though this is entirely unreasonable.

My wife immediately checks over the fleshy palm of our son, holding it firmly in hers, then rotating it as though it's as delicate as the china. *Everything's going to be okay*, she says to him; *everything's going to be okay*. Then I watch her stoop down to embrace him; his little head drooping onto her shoulder and furrowing at the brow. My wife becomes angry at the pieces; she points at them, saying how terrible they are to have done such a thing, but our son points too, causing my wife to laugh, and then him to giggle in her arms; his chunky body already struggling to break free, sure that she will follow him.

Without a thought, she sweeps up each broken piece of china and discards them outside, away from little hands, before joining our son in a game of chase. I wait a while; I watch as she feeds him; as she gazes at him indulging in every spoonful and pointing at the reflection from the shining silver as it dances around the room, fascinated as it flickers through the open window, like a firefly. He flaps his arms, convinced that he might also fly, amazed at his own potential, and colour rises into my wife's cheeks as she can't help but smile; the recent wrinkles by the sides of her eyes pulling more tightly together the longer she watches him. It is here that I take my leave and the grey army of grief follows me outside, in single file.

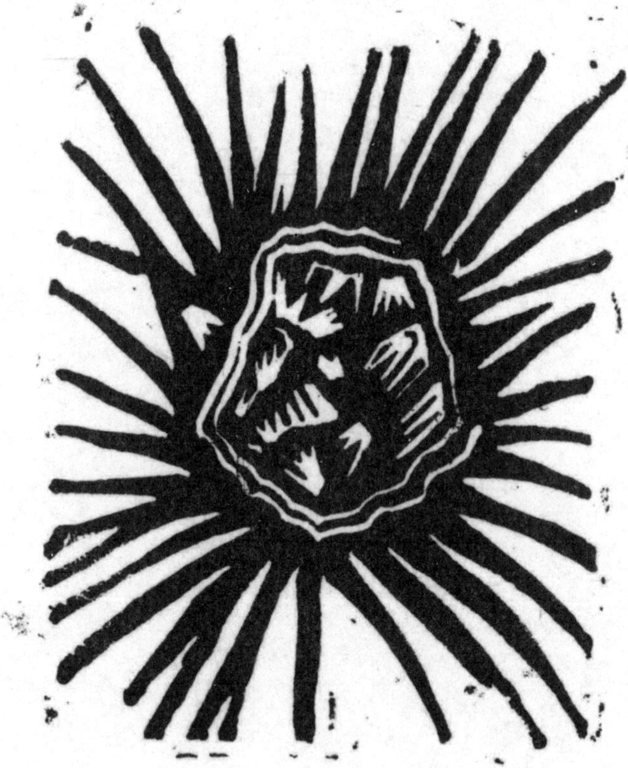

Diving for Starters

Siân Melangell Dafydd

Last autumn his lifeline took a turn. Many turns. There it is, the same line but interrupted by what happened to him that day and what lodged there inside his left palm. We don't know what it might mean for the course of his life. We wait.

In Marseille there is a street café. Nobody sits inside. The tables are on the pavement in a row in front of the fountain and the market where we buy little biscuits made with almond flour. The building is pink and so, so delicate – well, it might go in a puff. The windows are slim. They shut with off-black shutters – once, a long time ago, green, I'd say. You sense the white lace hanging behind and maybe someone watching. This is where we started off, last year, too.

We were there for the urchins. Let me tell you about those. It was the end of the season and we were almost too late. In any case, we arrived hopeful. Marseille was a long, long way to go for lunch, but sometimes you up-and-go without giving things much thought. This was one of those occasions. My grandparents used to talk of a trip they took by ferry to Ireland, just for the day, mind you, because it promised sunshine that side of the Irish Sea and they'd had just about enough of the rain. And my parents once 'popped' to Paris from London to eat oysters for lunch where Hemingway did – the Eurostar had opened a few weeks before and they wanted to prove it was do-able. They were in their own bed by eleven fifteen that night. Do-able. Yes, sometimes we do these things. No need to explain why. Just a *shall we?*

I'll say this much: we were there for the sea urchins. The Mistral was threatening. Le Mistral, le Mistral: it could be heard in every conversation under the terrace parasols. But we hadn't yet felt it so it was hard to believe. What we felt was early morning heat on our bare toes, from the sun and from the pavement. Soon, we'd be in the Mediterranean, the two of us, after filling up on almond biscuits and caffeine.

The spot we found was an almost-beach in a village he knew. A little bit out, not on the main road. I don't know. I could never find it again. There were three wooden fishing boats with oars: green, blue, brown. That's not much help, is it? Strange how it seemed sweltering hot on the café terrace. Two hours later, naked thighs on a stone, it seemed less so. But the water was just about warm enough. We abandoned our clothes on a boulder. I folded mine and he bundled his. Toes first. The sand, at least, was warm.

So, we were there for lunch and our starters were meant to be sea urchins, the main course, pomegranate. That's it. Neither of which we were guaranteed to find, too late for one and too early for the other, maybe – and neither of which showed any sign of showing up, but we'd travelled 500 km for them. Hope, hope. It wasn't time yet though. First things first: a bit of fun. We settled in and got ourselves wet.

* * *

When the hunt started, he was more successful than I was, with reason. I had never seen him this way. He wasn't agile by nature but now he was. This explains why he urged me to come, and why even I ended up thinking – well yes, why not, we'll just go.

I didn't see them. I wouldn't have seen them. Not if he wasn't at my side. But there they were, part of the current, part of the shade near a wall of rock down there. We had a glove each to protect us from the little mites, and held a net in the other hand. We dove below the level of our snorkel. He could hold his breath long enough to make me anxious. To the surface, spit, blow salt out of our noses – he'd found five and I had one. Again, red eyes this time – eight for him, three for me. And my hair got into my eyes and his did not.

It wasn't meant to be that way all morning. I came back up for air with ten. That was something. Then I counted to ten and there was no sign. Simple. What I didn't know was that if the sea looked the same on the surface, it wasn't behaving the same below and he was down there, below, in the thick of the difference. He was down there long enough for me to wonder, at least I knew it wasn't meant to be *this* way. I placed my face flat to the seawater and looked through the scratchy surface of the goggles. Oh he was there, he was seaweed, sort of swaying, yet in control of his body. A turmoil of underwater waves crashed him against the rock but that was fine. He reached out, pushed himself away and kicked to come up for air. See, things were going to be fine.

Another thing I didn't know: his hand, in reaching out for anything solid, met a sea urchin. He held it, squeezed it, and pushed himself up for air. His hand came up first, then elbow, his nose, a long, long breath and then an Ah. In his palm were the protective spines of an urchin, smashed into the flesh. One or two of them seemed to still twitch.

That's why I want to tell you about these sea urchins. They have roughly spherical bodies, with five equally-sized parts radiating out from the central axis. Their outer shell is covered with spines, black. These, if you look closely, move slowly. The body, below the spines, is not still. Inside, it has five parts, like the five parts of a hand, then.

* * *

The meal, then, with one of us injured. You cut a sea urchin in half with special sea-urchin scissors made to cut a round, two-inch ball, clean through without you having to get your hands anywhere near it. Inside, flesh in five parts. For this you need a spoon. We slopped them onto fresh bread full of air and a thick crust. Then I noticed.

The spines of the urchin in my mouth were still wiggling as though it hadn't caught on to the fact that it had in fact been slaughtered, halved and had its insides scooped out. I noticed the slow slow wince when my teeth were already in. I still think this is glorious. It was on the rock. The rock glistened with some geological sparks I knew nothing about and drops of water, drying. The two urchin halves twitched enough to walk a bit away from each other along the boulder. I chewed, filled myself with life. I am alright, here, I thought.

But that was then and this is now. And we know something isn't quite as it was. We drink these bloody coffees. I don't understand the affection we have for other people's scars but I know I love his hand. I remember my grandmother telling me to be careful of splinters. They were always wood, except for these urchin ones. He calls them glass. I don't see how that could be true. But glass splinters he says. I don't know if I believe him. Splinters, none the less. And according to my grandmother you need to be very, very wary of those. They wind their way from the flesh into the bloodstream and from there to the heart. There they puncture a second time though fatally. I don't know if I should trust my grandmother on that one.

* * *

For the main course: we had whatever the shoreline provided. Yes, pomegranate. Yes, we were lucky. Some were splitting already, they were so full. He gave instructions again. Suck the seeds. Spit the flesh into your palm (urchin spines or not), swallow the juice and throw the pulp. And so I was initiated. I belonged. And he was claimed by the sea. By then, the urchin spines had grown red sores each. Yes, he said, it hurt. He ate with his right hand and kept his left hand pressed against his chest, cool from seawater.

* * *

This autumn, we've returned to Marseille and his hand still has these black needle points – the last lives of one sea urchin. He says they twitch in there, he swears, itches, sweats. I doubt if this is possible. Surely they stop wincing eventually? Anyway, I scratch and pummel his palm while we drink our coffees and rip croissants.

Where are we going – I want to ask him, but I'm interrupted. A woman selling cat's eye shells passes by, the same colour as the dry walls around us, and asks if I'm reading his palm, his future. Not really, I say. I am reading last autumn and now we choose to remember the sun.

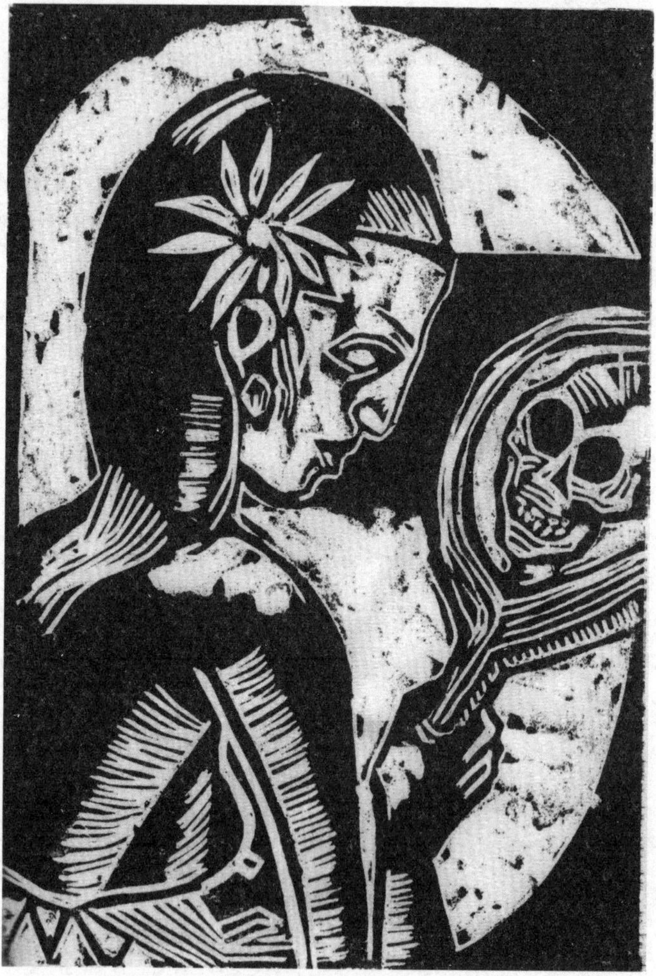

Sound Waves

Lane Ashfeldt

SHAY LOVES THE DARKNESS when he arrives in the studio each morning, says he hears better in the dark. His mum asks how he can stand to be locked away in the pitch black all summer. But it doesn't matter to Shay because he's doing what he loves. True, the money is rubbish. He's on the bottom rung, about on a level with a roadie, but when the last session of the day is done he has the chance to record his own songs. And he takes every chance he gets. Often, by the time he gets home, the dinner his mum cooked for him is shrivelled and the sun is long gone from the sky.

But the day he finds out about the festival, the sun is blindingly bright. Flying ants are swerving little waltzes in the air, on his shirt, on his arm, like he isn't even there. Shay swats them away and pulls out his mobile phone. It's his lunch break and he has been too busy all morning to answer it: humping gear, plugging instruments into amps, tracking the sound guy's every move so as to learn how to mix. Four new messages. He squints against the light to read the sender names. One from a club he's stopped going to, one each from Ellie and Matt.

Oh, and one from the festival. Himself, Ellie and Matt applied to work there because the tickets were sold out. It was Ellie's idea. She said if you did a few hours' work you'd get in free. They're still waiting to hear back.

An ant lands on the phone screen. Shay flicks it off and dodges into the corner shop. He fetches a cheese sandwich from the fridge and sets it on the counter. Then he reads the message: *Good news, you're in. You will work two shifts…* blah blah, he skips that bit, *and at all other times you will be free to enjoy the festival.* Perfect.

He sticks his card in the machine, ready to pay.

'There's a one-pound fee on transactions under a fiver,' the bloke behind the counter reminds him. Shay adds a drink and a few packs of chewing gum, pushing his bill up to £5.29. While the card is being processed he forwards the festival message to Ellie and Matt, adding, *Yours come thru?* Then he opens their messages and sees they're asking him the same thing. Score!

On the way back to work he's not bothered by the ants or the plastic taste of his cheese sandwich: all he's thinking is what a cool time they'll have at the festival.

LIVI IS FINDING it hard to focus on the music. Last night she couldn't sleep. She went downstairs and munched half a dozen chocolate biscuits, and this morning her jeans wouldn't zip up. A bad start to the day, one that feeds her fears of being too old for this line of work. At 37, she feels older. Her teenage daughter thinks she's low on rock-star attitude, and has said so. Which doesn't help. But her daughter doesn't get the whole playing live thing. Never has, in spite of her gift for music. It's not up to you when you stop playing – not if you're in a band that the fans still want to hear. And thank Christ for small mercies, Livi thinks, at least I'm only on bass. Far worse to be up front under the spotlight, like Moro.

It's years since the Fa So Las toured or made a new album. Herself and Moro turned down a few gigs recently but when the festival offered them a headline slot, their manager insisted. 'Look girls, it's not Glasto, but it's very influential,' he said. 'Yous are lucky to be asked. Just get a haircut, go on a diet maybe, and yous'll have a great time.'

Livi looks at her stomach, half hidden by the bass. She gains weight when she's stressed and has gone up a clothes size this past month. In contrast the session musicians who took over the vacant slots on drums and guitar are tall and thin in a retro, junkie sort of way. Next to them she's like a cartoon Jack Sprat's wife. The heat in the studio's getting to her, but the two Jack Sprats haven't a hair out of place between them.

Sweat makes her fingers slip on a key change. She stops playing and waits for the next in-point, but Moro cuts the song.

'Li-vee! What's with you? The run-through's for the benefit of the new guys, not the old hands.'

'Sorry.'

'Want to carry on?'

'Sure. Shall we go again from the chorus?'

'No, take it from the top.'

Moro counts them in again and Livi does her best not to feel belittled. Familiar chords start up: the opening bars of a song that made them a million back in the days when a million counted for something, and Livi finds that if she closes her eyes and stops worrying, her fingers know exactly where they need to be.

ELLIE, MATT AND HIMSELF leave for the festival early on the Thursday. The train is like any train, but when they board the boat to the island and are surrounded by other festival-goers, there's a real sense of anticipation. The sea is calm, the water flat. Too flat almost, but then this is only a strait – the real sea is on the far side of the island. The wild side. As he watches the mainland recede, Shay has the feeling they are leaving reality behind. The festival is another world, a world of games and music and dressing up. A place where anything can happen.

THEY HAVE BACKSTAGE PASSES for the whole weekend and Livi is curious to hear the other bands, but Moro decides they're to keep away until the last minute. 'We need to be on form,' she says. 'Hanging around in a crowd could put us off our stride.'

On the Friday they do one last rehearsal. The whole set is pretty tight by now, those early disasters with timing all ironed out. Afterwards Livi and Moro go to a spa and get facials, a massage, new haircuts. Livi wonders how come she never noticed when they were starting out that so much of the music business is not about music at all.

'Got to look the part,' Moro says.

To Livi's relief she picks up the tab: royalties have been low this last couple of years, and Moro does earn the most, after all, because she co-wrote their hits.

ALONG WITH the two-man cowboy print teepee which all three of them have somehow squeezed into, Ellie brought tonnes of dried fruit, rice cakes, even fresh fruit. Matt's contribution is a backpack filled with vodka cocktails, siphoned into juice bottles to get past security. All Shay packed was his guitar and a skimpy sleeping bag last used at scouts. It's late in the morning and Matt, Shay, and their camping neighbours are dozing in the sun on a small patch of grass between the tents, while Ellie tidies out the teepee. Watching her plump up the pillow on her sleeping bag, Shay smiles. Chalk and cheese, her and Matt.

Ellie shrugs as she comes outside. 'Had to bring it. Can never get to sleep without a pillow.'

'Sleep?' Matt says. 'It's the last thing that should be on your mind this weekend.'

The blokes from the next tent laugh. One of them taps the girl next to him who is stretched on a sleeping bag, sunning herself.

'Hear that, gorgeous? Think you're getting any beauty sleep this weekend? You're out of luck.'

The girl briefly lifts one of her pink headphones. 'I didn't catch that.' When the only response is laughter, she pops the phones back on and finger-dances in an infectious, good humoured way.

Matt grins and rolls on to his back. 'Brilliant. I'm telling you, this is gonna be the most brilliant weekend of your life.'

LIVI'S BEEN FASTING all week, and has on a flattering pair of stretch jeans. There's a weird vibe backstage. A kind of invisible wall has grown up between the two session musicians, and herself and Moro. Added to this there's a whole separate war going on between Moro and the other headline act: a jostle for power over start times, set-ups, who has the most gear on stage, that sort of thing. Moro keeps telling anyone who'll listen that the other band are total divas. Livi tries not to get involved.

'Just going out for a few, get some air.'

Moro says, 'Don't be long.'

SHAY TENDS to take Matt's predictions with a barrowload of salt so he's surprised now to be thinking, maybe Matt's right and this really is going to be the best weekend ever. They haven't had to work too hard: they did a session on the gates on Friday, taking tickets and fixing bracelets on the newbies. Last night he was up till three at a small outlying venue, the Chapel, jamming and partying and talking shop with other young musicians. It's late in the afternoon, the hiatus before the evening bands begin, and he's sitting on the grass, sunburned and grubby, strumming his guitar.

Every afternoon so far he has eaten at the bus cafe before going to catch the bands, but today he's broke so he's making do with one of Matt's juice bottles. Not the smartest way in the world to start the evening, he learns, as vodka scalds his throat.

He glances at the girl with the pink headphones, who works in the cafe. Late last night she turned up at the Chapel. Easily the high point of his entire festival. Only a handful of people were left on the dance-floor, dwindling to just the two of them for the last song. When the music ended they walked back to camp together and kissed, before zipping themselves into their separate tents. A big part of why he's so tired right now is because afterwards he couldn't stop thinking about her.

Today the girl's pink headphones dangle round her neck as she takes coffee orders. She shows no sign of having seen Shay arrive, but on her break she brings over two coffees and a flapjack and sits beside him.

'Hey. You look like you could use some sustenance.'

He bites into the flapjack. 'Cheers. Get you back later. You going up to the Chapel tonight?'

'Might do.' She shrugs. 'Got to eat a proper dinner at some point, or I'll be ill.' Shay is surprised.

She looks such a festival insider, and he's beginning to buy into Matt's line that the only way to get through a festival is to take the marathon approach and put selected physical maintenance – sleeping, eating, and washing, for example – on hold until it's over.

'Don't they feed you here?'

'Sure, but my friend Julie who cooks at the Undersea Tavern has asked a few friends around tonight for a midnight feast. Sounds great – South Sea Soup, Seafaring Spaghetti, Shipwreck Pavlova with Salted Caramel.'

Shay looks away. Suddenly the attraction of the Chapel has palled. Not so much because of the food: he just wants to be wherever she is going to be.

ADRIFT IN THE CROWD, Livi forgets her promise to return to the backstage area. Streams and eddies of people carry her over hills sloped like sine waves, dotted with marquees and small stages that each throw out a different sound. When she comes to the woods she follows a looping pathway between tall shadowy trees. In a clearing by the lake, thirty or so people are dancing around an outsized jukebox. But the music doesn't sound pre-recorded, and sure enough when Livi looks closer she sees half a dozen musicians crammed inside, playing and singing live. They have an incredible range: disco, punk, ska, reggae, old, new, happy, sad.

Somehow hearing the jukebox musicians crank out rowdy, danceable versions of songs written decades ago gives her a fresh take on the Fa So Las. The sound of any individual band is just one drop in this tidal ebb and flow, this push and pull, this ocean of musics that makes one song popular this year, another the next.

So what if the Fa So Las scored a slot this year only because a younger, more fashionable band named their early hits as an influence? The fact they've been around awhile is nothing to be ashamed of. Music doesn't stand still, it is all about change. Right now their sound has floated up to the surface. Soon it will be drowned out again by other new sounds flowing into the mix. They may as well bask in the moment: celebrate.

A text from Moro summons her backstage.

AT THE END of their set an exhausted Livi and Moro do the backstage meet-and-greets, then make their way to the Undersea Tavern. The crowd loved them, and that's enough for Livi. Even Moro seems happy. As they move through the hordes they notice that the festival punters are wearing fancy dress tonight: jellyfish and sharks, umbrellas dangling octopus legs, swordfish, stingrays, sea urchins. On the grass outside the tavern a few young musicians are playing. The guitarist stops when he sees them, and comes over.

'Hi, I caught your show earlier. You were amazing.'

Moro says there's someone inside that she must catch up with. Livi smiles and thanks the young guitarist.

'Your whole sound really influenced me a lot when I was young,' he adds.

Livi tries not to laugh at the when I was young bit, because he looks as if he's somewhere between the ages of sixteen and nineteen.

'It's still quite influential. To me, anyway,' she jokes.

He asks her about the lead guitar chords to one of their early hits, 'Saturday Night'. Livi isn't sure, but offers to play him the bass section to help work it out. Someone hands her a bass guitar and they start jamming.

WHEN THE GIRL with the pink headphones arrives, Shay doesn't notice at first because she's under one of those umbrellas with lights dangling from it. A jellyfish costume. He and the Fa So Las bassist are sitting cross-legged on the floor playing softly. They've nearly got the whole song, there's just one rogue chord they haven't managed to nail. When he sees the girl looking down at them, Shay thinks she's upset. He starts guiltily and stumbles to his feet. Looking at her clear skin, at the curve of her cheek, he's never been so alive, so completely in the now.

'Hey, I want you to meet Livi from the Fa So Las,' he says. 'This is…' And he feels stupid then, because he doesn't know her name. He has never thought to ask. Whenever she is near, she is simply more there than anyone else, almost as if she doesn't need a name.

'…Carlita, my daughter!' Livi says, laughing. 'We're both here for the supper tonight. Will you be coming to that as well?'

'Uh, I don't think, I mean…'

'It sounds fab, all the food is sea-flavoured to match the dress-up thing.'

Shay feels awkward: he looks at the girl. Carlita. The name seems wrong for her, somehow. Too frilly.

'We're all invited.' She whacks him lightly like they've known each other years, not days. 'You too. I asked Julie.'

In that second Shay knows he will be with this girl ten and twenty years from now. He sees the slight curve of her nose in profile, and he knows that over time this curve will become stronger, more like Livi's. And her body too will become more curvy in shape than it is now. To him this doesn't matter in the least, not so long as he can be with her to see it happen.

MATT HAS NEVER been to a music festival with a girlfriend before. It's different. Better in some ways. But one odd side-effect is things are a bit less haphazard than he feels festivals ought to be. He's used to being last man to crash, and this is no longer the case. For the second night running he's in his sleeping bag before Shay has even got back to base.

'Wonder what Shay is up to?'

'I thought he was doing his other shift.'

'No, he's on gates tomorrow for the exodus, poor sod. Still, you'd think he'd have sent us a text.'

'Perhaps his battery's flat. Anyway, he's bound to be back at some point. Probably wake us up,' Ellie says sleepily. Then, 'Say if he's not back by the time we've to pack up, what will we do with his stuff?'

'What stuff?'

He flicks the torch on the other side of the teepee. Not much there. Shay's been taking his guitar around with him in a backpack. The only thing left is that raggedy khaki sleeping bag he's had since they were in scouts.

ALL EVENING Shay has been thinking that what he wants most in the world is to be on his own with this girl. Carlita? Carla, maybe. But he can't think of anywhere to go where that is possible. They're both sharing tents with friends, and the festival is not geared up for privacy. In the end she is the one who does something about it. They're walking reluctantly back to the tents when she takes his hand and drags him in a different direction. He's not sure where they're headed until the curve of the double-decker bus looms, and he hears a jangle of keys.

'I'm on earlies tomorrow, so they gave me a key. I reckon the best plan tonight is to stay here.'

There's a pause. She is on the platform, one foot on the stairs. Shay hesitates on the grass outside. She turns.

'You going or staying?'

He leaps aboard and curls his arm around her waist. 'Given the option – I'm staying, of course.'

'Good.'

IT'S MAD BUSY AT THE PIER the day they leave. Ferries, catamarans, hovercraft – anything that floats has been pressed into service to run an island-to-mainland shuttle from six in the morning till whenever it takes. No one's sure exactly how many thousands of people need to get off the island, but it's a big number. Ellie and Matt pack up at dawn and manage to get themselves on a train home by lunchtime. Shay and the girl still haven't left the campsite by then. She is on brunch duty and he is working a shift on the gates. By the time they finally board a boat to the mainland, it's gone seven.

The boat is small and old fashioned, the elderly crew more used to taking retired couples on harbour tours than shunting music fans across the Solent. Out of habit the skipper steers one-handed and calls out the sights into his microphone. Few of the passengers bother to go on deck and look. Most gather indoors where the comfy seats are, sleeping, or trying to. A guy Shay knows from the sessions at the Chapel mutters,

'What's with the history lesson? We don't need this right now.'

Carla smiles weakly.

Shay is so tired he won't be able to sleep tonight. Maybe he's forgotten how to do sleep. They go outside.

The stairs to the top deck wobble underfoot and Shay realises it's not the sea but his own exhaustion making them move. The sea is dotted with forts from forgotten Anglo-Saxon battles that make sense only to the boat's captain. The sight of land is unwelcome: it means the return of the routine, sensible, everyday world.

'I'm going back inside, I'm barely able to stand up.' Carla gestures to his guitar. 'Want me to look after that?'

'It's fine,' Shay says.

It's almost like the guitar is part of him, he can barely feel it any more, but so she knows he trusts her with it and to keep her with him a moment longer he says, 'Actually, yeah, go on, then,' and shrugs off the backpack.

In this area of the top deck there are no seats, no one near enough to hear them, and he kisses her on the forehead and says shyly, 'I think I love you.'

She hugs him hard, as if conscious this may not be possible when they reach the train station on the other side, and mumbles into his chest: 'I know.'

For a moment after she has gone below, Shay feels thrown. Does her answer mean she isn't into him? No. It means, do things at your own pace, try not to rush. But it's hard not to feel rushed. They haven't talked much about what will happen back on the mainland, but it won't be easy to stay in touch. Aside from living in different cities, they both live with their parents. And his mum is way less cool than Livi: no way would she let a girl he has just met stay over. But Carla has said, 'If you think it's any different at mine, you've not met my dad.'

Shay is too shattered right now to see a way round

this, but there has to be a way. This thing between them, it's important. Put something real like this on hold, let it fizzle out into nothing, and imagine how bad you'd feel. Very. It's like the start of a song that hasn't got going yet. It needs time. They need time.

On the starboard side they must be close to land, for the captain is pointing out the place where they used to load convicts onto prison ships bound for Australia. This side, Shay sees only dusky light on the water. He slips his mobile phone out of his pocket. The last shot he took is a close-up of Carla. He wants a matching shot of himself, now, before the glitter and the dirt have rubbed off, as a souvenir of the weekend they first met. There's just enough battery. He clambers on a railing, holds up the phone so the evening sky and the sea will show behind him.

He clicks.

As he's checking to see if the picture came out, the phone slips. He twists his leg, manages to bounce it off his knee so it lands on deck. Phew, one and a half thousand photos saved. And all his numbers.

Then it happens: his feet lose their grip on the rails. He tilts back. In a second he's in a mid-air reverse somersault, like an Olympic show diver but less controlled. He doesn't call out, there's no time for fear, he's just focused on getting out of this. He's thinking it'll be okay right up to the second when the sea beneath him vanishes, replaced by an intense orange mist as his head meets the side of the boat. Dark shapes crowd out the orange, like when he was a small child pushing thumbs on his eyelids to block out the sun. Then the shapes are gone, and after this Shay is not thinking any more. He does not sense the slick, cold water that opens up, takes hold and softly closes around him. He does not hear the boat chug on without him. He does not even feel the water fill up his air passages, making him more and more heavy until his body gently sinks below the surface.

CARLA IS ASLEEP when the boat comes to land. She stirs, looks around her at the empty seats, confused, and packs up her things. A crew member watches from nearby, arm raised to indicate the exit route. Where is he? She struggles to lift both her backpack and his guitar. When she reaches the gangplank and finds he's not there she tells the officer, 'My friend, he's up top. He wouldn't leave without me. See – I've got his guitar.'

But the officer blocks her way. 'There's no one up there, love. We always do a headcount, and you're last off.'

Carla is stunned. She can't believe Shay would walk away like this. He really didn't seem the type.

She traipses up the ramp to the train station. No sign of him. And she hasn't got his phone number, so she can't send a text to find out where he is. She hurries back, convinced it's a mistake. He's probably curled up asleep somewhere. She'll make them let her on, buy a ticket if she has to. But by the time she reaches the dock, crowds of people are pouring off a huge ferry and the small boat they crossed on is making its way back to the island.

LIVI WORRIES ABOUT her daughter. This autumn she started her final year of school, but in the weeks since the festival she has been fragile and withdrawn. She stays in her room, rarely going out except for school. When Livi asks what's wrong she swears it's nothing, it's just that no one is going out this year because of the exams.

'Listen, Carlita, I'm worried about you. Don't you trust me enough to tell me what the problem is?'

No reply. Is it something Livi did, or something she failed to do? They were both at the festival when all this started. Perhaps she should have told her daughter not to work that last day, and given her a lift home with the band. And there's that boy Carlita was talking to the last night. But he had seemed such a nice boy.

'Tell me, is this about your guitar player?'

'What guitar player?'

'The one who asked me the chords to "Saturday Night". You remember, at the Undersea Tavern.'

'I met a lot of people at the festival, I don't remember them all now.'

She does remember, Livi's sure of it.

'Isn't that his guitar in your room?'

'Oh, that. I bought it off someone at the festival who was short of the train fare home.'

There is a tightness to her daughter's voice that tells Livi it's best to keep out. She has learned the hard way that sometimes this is what she must do.

Carlita hasn't played guitar in a long time. Five or six years. Not since Livi put her up for a school music scholarship. As a child she was a natural, but the day of her audition she asked Livi to stay away. They've never discussed what happened that day. All she knows is, she got no scholarship, and later dropped all music lessons.

Now Livi changes the subject to what's for dinner. She knows better than to bring up the topic again, but one day when her daughter is at school she takes the guitar out of its canvas pack. It sounds just like the one she remembers the boy playing. Looks the same, too.

Still Livi keeps her silence. Even when, as she returns home from an evening out, she hears guitar music coming from upstairs. This happens several times over the next weeks, the music always stopping as soon as she's through the door, and Livi learns to pause before putting her key in the lock. The songs her daughter plays are not ones she has heard before. They are new. Some are happy, some sad; but that is okay. The important thing is she's playing again.

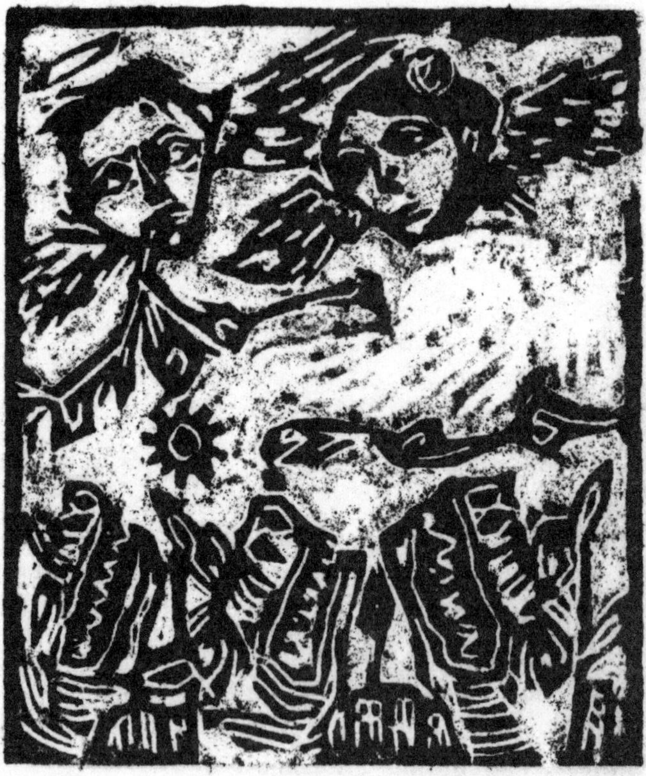

Meringue

Craig Hawes

It's my turn at Scrabble and everyone's waiting for me. I pretend not to realise, just to wind them up a bit.

I want to go to the amusement arcade to get away from Corinne, my bitch of a sister, but I spent all my money there on the first day of the holiday. Dad went ape, so there's more chance of me sprouting wings than getting a few quid out of him now.

I can't remember being so bored. *Ever*. Dad tells me to read one of my comics, but I can only read so much before the letters start jumping and crossing and my head spins like a yo-yo.

'Go *on*, Gav,' says Corinne, sucking in her cheeks, like she always does when she's about to say something really sarcastic. 'You never know, you might be able to make the word *merinjew.*'

Here we go again.

My father smirks and my mother picks up a letter tile

and presses it to her pursed lips, as if it's a plug to stop the laughter escaping. When she realises it's an M she can't help herself, and suddenly the three of them are in hysterics.

This has been the big joke of the holiday. Last week, at a restaurant in town, I was wondering aloud which dessert to have and pronounced 'meringue' wrong. Like *that* all of a sudden makes me stupid. Corrine, as I knew she would, milked it to the max.

'My brother says he wants the *merinjew*,' she said to the waitress. 'Do you think the chef knows how to make *merinjew*s?' Worst thing was, the waitress laughed too. I wouldn't have *given* a shit if it was some wrinkly old biddy, but she looked just like Miley Cyrus, so I tried to imagine my face packed in ice – freezing numb – to stop it going red like it does when the teachers ask me stuff in class and I get the wrong answer. But this time it doesn't work.

I try to think of something horrible to say back to Corinne but she's concentrating on her new mobile phone, sending poison texts to some unknown enemy. I'd love to make her cry, but she's way cleverer than me, always ready with a smart-arse reply. And this always makes me madder than ever. Sometimes I swear I'd like to slap her fat face, ram a big bloody *merinjew* into it, like they do with custard pies on the telly.

Thank God I haven't been stuck with her the whole holiday. She's spent most of the week hanging around on another part of the site, where the tents are, with two 'really cool' sisters from Scotland. At least that's what she told us. We never saw them, not even once.

I study my letters, hopelessly.

'What's the matter, dopey, stuck are you?' says Corrine, looking up from her phone.

'Oh, just help him, Dad, or he'll take till flippin' Christmas.'

'I don't need any help,' I say to Corinne. 'So shut your fat face.'

'Enough bickering,' says my mother, staring up at the grey clouds as if she can hypnotise them into parting for the sun. Dad takes a couple of empty tea cups into the caravan and Corinne, seizing her chance, sticks two fingers up at me – not that my parents would bother to say anything if they caught her.

Corinne is flavour of the month right now because she's just started a weekend job in a florists. My parents say she is 'enterprising'. I on the other hand am a 'lazy little sod' because I refuse to get a paper round. But I'm not lazy, I just have other plans. My dream is to draw the pictures in superhero comics, but first I need to find someone to write the words that go into the speech bubbles. My superhero's power will be teleportation and he'll be able to appear anywhere in the world just by shutting his eyes and wishing it. He'll take holidays in places like Disney World and Japan – not Lakeview Caravan Park in rainy Wales that's for sure.

Corinne got a job because she wants to buy a car when she turns seventeen next year. The girls in her year have started to go off with older boys with flashy wheels – lots of gleaming chrome and spoilers and booming sound systems that you can hear fifty streets away. Corinne's one of the girls who gets left behind on the bus stop because she isn't slim and pretty like most of her so-called friends. I know this because Rhys Thurston in my year has an older brother who hangs with the cool car crowd and he told Rhys and Rhys told me. Hearing this, I didn't know whether it made me happy or sad.

Dad comes out of the caravan, digging into his jeans pockets, and I hear the clink of coins. He pulls out two fistfuls for inspection, puts the silver and gold ones back in his pocket, and beckons me over.

No one says anything but the Scrabble game seems to have been abandoned. I'm glad.

Corinne was destroying me.

I cup my hands like a beggar and receive the bounty, all two-pence pieces and a few ones, some covered in that yucky green fuzz that clings to old coins like seaweed on rocks.

'Last of the big spenders, eh, Dad?'

'Oi, cheeky! Bagsy ten percent of any winnings,' he says, winking.

The last thing I hear as I run toward the amusement arcade is Corinne telling Dad that I'll come back with nothing.

The amusement arcade has four slot machines, three video games and a pool table with baize that is torn in places and threadbare, like our school football pitch at the end of the season. There are three boys about Corinne's age around the table. Two of them are in the middle of a game while the other one leans against the wall drinking from a plastic Coke bottle. Probably contains something stronger than Coke, though, the way he clenches his teeth after every swig.

I choose a slot machine that is two-pence per credit and load it up with twenty-six pence – thirteen credits. Thirteen's my age. A good sign I hope.

Three melons is the jackpot – three pounds fifty – but I can't even get three oranges, which would win me thirty pence. When I get two bells, which is ten pence, I take the money instead of hitting the flashing double-or-nothing button. The machine plays an ice cream van jingle then spits out the coins into the metal trough below. At least I can carry on playing for a bit longer. I tell myself that if I win the jackpot I'll go back to the caravan with ginormous ice creams for everyone, maybe even Corinne, just to see the look on her face.

One by one, I slide the five coins out of the trough and stack them in my hand.

'Don't spend it all at once,' shouts over one of the boys as he lines up a shot. He's mixed-race with an accent like they have in *Coronation Street*. He wears a Man United football top and jeans with loads of pockets.

The other two boys laugh. The one standing against the wall with the Coke bottle is blonde, the other one dark-haired. They're dressed more surfy, with bright T-shirts and long baggy shorts.

I'm down to my last four credits on the machine when something lands onto the floor beside me. It's the cue ball, which has somehow leapt off the table and rolled next to my foot. By the time I pick it up, the dark-haired boy is standing beside me holding out his hand. I give him the ball and he says, 'Thanks, mate.' As he turns, I notice a raspberry-coloured mark on his neck. The same kind of mark the teachers at school make you cover up with a blue sticking plaster. After end of term discos it's worst. You'd swear our school had some sort of vampire problem. It's like a badge of honour for the year elevens.

The boys finish their game and lark about. They do kung fu moves with the cue-sticks. The blonde one is drunk and steadies himself against the side of the table. There are coins lined up on the side cushion to show they haven't finished playing.

'We could play doubles,' says the boy in the Man United shirt.

'Not in his state we can't,' says the dark-haired boy, jerking his head at the drunk blonde boy. 'No way I'm gonna be *his* partner.'

'Oi, you, you got any mates?' says Man United, looking in my direction.

I look around the arcade, but there's no one else in sight.

Man United laughs. 'Yeah, you. Got any mates? Two of us against two of you.'

'I'm here with my family,' I say. 'I don't really know anyone else.'

'Your dad then, go and get him, go on. We'll beat anyone, we're the fucking business, we are.'

'He doesn't really like pool.'

'Brother, sister...?'

'Well, I've got a sister, but she doesn't play either.'

I look at the slot machine and realise I'm all out of turns – and money. I wander over to the pool table, hoping they'll give me a game, partner or not.

'How old's your sister, then?' says the dark-haired boy. 'Fit is she?'

The other two laugh.

'She's sixteen,' I say.

'What's her name?' says Man United.

'Corinne,' I say.

'Corinne?' says the dark-haired boy, placing his pool cue on the table. 'Long brown hair, blue eyes, bit sort of, uh, chubby, like?'

They're all looking at each other like they know some dark secret.

I shrug my shoulders.

'Bet your mum don't need no vacuum cleaner when her daughter can do that,' says Man United, pointing at the blonde boy with the love-bite.

'This isn't all she's sucked, though, right, Cootsy?' laughs the blonde boy.

Grinning, Man United plays the end of his cue into a small rip in the baize.

'Yeah, we've all had a poke in her pockets,' says the dark-haired boy, and the next thing I know he's sitting on his backside clutching his face.

When he takes his hands away, I see a trickle of blood coming out of his nose. It looks fake and almost black, like the molasses my mother makes cookies with. But then it's the first time I've seen so much blood so close up. Come to think of it, it's the first time I've ever hit anyone too.

His two friends gawp at me as if I've just transformed from Clark Kent into Superman, and suddenly I'm outside the arcade, running through the drizzle towards our caravan. I hear angry shouts behind me, but I keep on running and running over the wet grass, between caravans and tents, ducking under makeshift washing lines, hurdling over guy ropes. When I look behind me, I can't see the three boys anywhere and I'm close to our pitch now.

I walk when I get near, calmly, as if nothing has happened. The awning has been taken in and I see that the car is attached to the caravan. Corinne is already sitting in the backseat so I open the door and climb in next to her.

'Yuck! Your hand,' she says.

I look down and notice that my knuckles are grazed and there's blood, though not much.

She gives me a weird look, then tuts and shakes her head.

As we drive through the site on the way out, my father asks me how much I won on the fruit machines. He cracks some daft joke about how everyone was relying on me to buy the petrol for the journey home, but only mum laughs.

We pass the amusement arcade. Outside the three boys are kicking an empty beer can against the wall. The dark-haired one has white tissue paper fanning out of his nostril. It looks like a small bird has tried to fly up his nose and got stuck. For the seconds it takes to pass them Corinne hides her face by playing with her hair, but they've spotted us and shout something as we pass, laughing and making rude gestures.

'Friends of yours, Gavin?' my mother says, studying them in the wing-mirror. 'I sincerely hope not.'

'*No* friends of *mine*, mum,' I say, glancing across at Corinne, whose face is turning bright red.

She folds her arms across her chest and stares at the back of dad's seat.

I am thrilled by the silence.

'Mum?' I ask, staring at Corinne. 'Do you believe in vampires?'

'*Vampires*? What on *earth* are you asking me that for?' she laughs.

'Reckon this campsite was full of them.'

'You and your bloody comics,' chuckles my father.

Corinne winds down the window and tilts her head to catch the breeze.

'It's not *that* warm,' I say.

An hour later, Corinne is fast asleep, her head resting against a rolled-up sweater that is pressed against the window. Her left hand rests on the seat between us. I notice the scar on her little finger where she cut herself falling off her little pink Barbie bike while carrying me on the handlebars – back when we were small, when I was proud of her for being the only kid on our street who could ride a bike without stabilisers. When she grew too big for it she painted it bright red with Dad's help and gave it to me. I never rode it, but she didn't seem to mind. I can't remember when we stopped being friends. Or why.

I place my little finger on top of Corinne's – the one with the scar – and one big blue eye slides open to look at me. I expect her to pull her hand away, but she doesn't. I feel her little finger curl around mine, like a caterpillar around a flower stalk, and her eye closes shut. There's the flicker of a smile on a face that is budding, I can see now, into something quite beautiful.

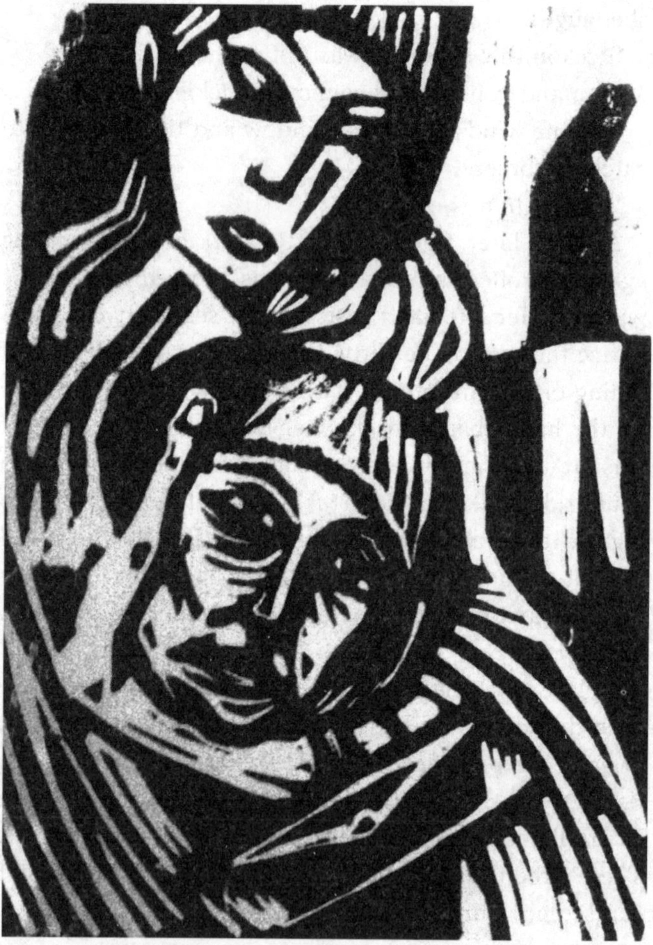

Oku Hanafu

Eluned Gramich

It is Oku Hanafu's last performance at the Kabukiza Theatre in Tokyo. Yoko stands at the entrance to the auditorium, pulling at a loose thread from her kimono. Her mother is next to her, the back of her wheelchair pressed up against the red walls, watching her daughter disapprovingly. Drawing the thread from her sleeve, Yoko tries to break it off, but succeeds only in unravelling it further. Please stop, says her mother, as if she can't bear to see the kimono so abused. She takes out a make-up case from her stringed purse and cuts the unruly thread with her nail scissors. Yoko submits, saying nothing.

'How long do we have to wait for?' asks her mother, replacing the utensils in her purse.

'Twenty minutes.'

Her mother sighs, 'I told you we should have gone to the matinee.'

Yoko has lived with her mother's impatience all her life. She knows it well and no longer bothers to acknowledge it. But tonight Yoko shares her mother's agitation; she can't sit down, scans the lobby with her eyes; she fidgets. Perhaps it's because it's already dark outside. And there is something wrong about being out of the house at night. Yoko remembers the last time she was out in the evening, six months ago. She had felt the same nervousness, the same heightened self-consciousness which borders on the unwell, like a hibernating animal woken in the middle of winter. Yoko could not imagine ever getting used to walking about at night like this, like other people, as if it were natural.

But it's not only the time of day which irks Yoko's mother. Yoko knows it's desire too. The old woman is in love, and the object of her affection is Oku Hanafu, the man who plays the female lead of the grand Kabuki plays. So handsome, she coos, handsome in and out of costume. Handsome and beautiful simultaneously. Oku Hanafu is the reason why Yoko's mother insisted on good tickets: in the stalls, the fourth row, and on the right side of the stage, allowing for the best view of the runway where the Kabuki actors dance their way from one world to the other. Yoko did as she was told, but to her mother's dismay, she chose the evening performance. The evening, Yoko said, promised a warmer atmosphere; and they'd be sure of catching the very last moments of Hanafu's long and illustrious career on the stage. Her mother complained – Won't it be very crowded? How shall we get home in the dark? – not because she nursed a particular fear of crowds or the dark, but because she was not used to her daughter making such abrupt and solitary decisions.

Yoko hovers around her mother, restless. She buys the programme, but her mother reads it, holding it close to her face because she refuses to wear reading glasses on account of her hair. The straps of Yoko's purse are wrapped tightly around her hands, cutting off the blood supply. The foyer is filling with people, some of whom Yoko recognises: regulars who, like them, come to the Kabuki theatre every month. Women of her mother's age. They exchange smiles, but Yoko keeps close to the wall, fearing conversations with acquaintances. Still, she watches Tokyo society filtering in with the cool springtime air. Husbands in suits, bowing to listen to their wives, the occasional student in bright casual wear, a bewildered Westerner invited along by well-meaning friends. People queue to order Bento boxes and champagne for the interval. Women buy glutinous rice cakes wrapped in cherry-leaves to take home to their children. Couples gaze at the photographs of the Kabuki actors, Oku Hanafu first among them. The noise level increases until Yoko finds that her heart is beating in her ears. Loud noises make her nervous. The straps of her bag tighten on her fine wrists.

The truth is Yoko is waiting for someone. She hasn't made any specific arrangement, but she knows he will keep the appointment, just as her mother knows the actor Oku Hanafu will keep his. The kind of people that are here – the western style dresses and heels, the chatter, the meeting and greeting – surely they are his people. The kind of people who don't live in the quiet, empty hours of the daytime, the kind of people who do not buy tickets for Matinees.

When he does arrive, shrugging the coat from his shoulders, he is not alone, but with a group of people. He is the last to enter. Yoku looks away, afraid he might catch her staring.

'Is that Torimitsu-San?' asks her mother, putting the programme to one side.

'Ten minutes until doors open,' says Yoko.

'It certainly is her. What a dreadful dress – such a dreary green. It makes her look like a pile of old tea leaves.'

Yoko examines the dress for herself, and he chooses that moment to look across. He catches her eye. There is a moment's hesitation before he smiles, but by that time she has already looked away.

'Will they come over I wonder,' says her mother. 'People always feel obliged to greet one another all the time, even when they have nothing to say to each other.'

'They won't come and greet us,' says Yoko bitterly, 'when there are so many other people to talk to.'

Yoko likes to review things carefully: the weather, train timetables, traffic reports, earthquake monitors, radiation readings. She separates her handbag into several plastic envelopes so that the lining does not get damaged or dirty. Whether she should wear her hair up or down, glasses or contact lenses, ice coffee or ice tea, such decisions make her sick with worry. She can't bear the smell of food to linger in the kitchen. She owns three vacuum cleaners of different manufacturers. She finds it so painful when motorbikes and other loud vehicles pass by that she often has to fight back tears.

But her nature is not all sensitivity. When the delivery man is late, she tells him off, even though she has nothing to do during the day. Once, in a Ginza department store, she returned a frying pan because it had been incorrectly labelled. The department store refused to refund her. Yoko took out her measuring tape and proved to the sneering manager that, in fact, the measurement on the label did not match the actual measurement of the pan and that she would not be leaving until they had provided a full refund.

On seeing him and his aunt, Torimitsu, moving towards them through the throng, this kind of bravery fails her. She becomes smaller with every step they take. She's suddenly gripped by uncertainty: unsure of how she fills the space, unsure whether she is a woman like all the other women around her, or a phantom looking through a funnel out onto the world. Torimitsu takes the helm. There are sweat marks on the green satin of her dress.

'You're here! Of course, it's Hanafu isn't it? The angel of the stage, they say he's not slept for a week. They say he can't apply his own make-up his hands are trembling so much!'

'Who says?' Her mother, outraged at the gossip. Outraged, too, no doubt, at Torimitsu's awful manners. Not even a formal "Good evening!" 'I heard that Hanafu always prepares alone in the green room,' her mother continues.

They bow in greeting; her mother apologising for not getting up.

'As you can see I have to be wheeled about in this contraption now,' she explains.

'Think nothing of it,' says Torimitsu with a worried glance at Yoko. She is surprised at how quickly my mother's worsened, thinks Yoko, and she's scared for herself. They are the same age, Torimitsu and my mother.

'And you must remember Nakamura-san, my nephew.'

He comes forward rather shyly, the man Yoko has been waiting for. Shoulders bowed apologetically; a collar too big for his thin throat, a fragile expression; his skin porcelain. But when he speaks, his words are clear and eloquent, unshaken by the situation. Still, he doesn't look at Yoko, not yet.

'You hear all sorts of stories about Hanafu. I'm sure we'll hear even more now he's retiring from the stage,' he says. 'It'll all come out of the woodwork.'

'Lies and slander,' says her mother.

'What kind of stories?' Yoko asks.

'Oh all sorts,' Torimitsu says dismissively. Yoko wonders why Torimitsu is suddenly so embarrassed.

'What sort of stories?' Yoko goes on, playing up, wanting to hear the words from the older woman's lips, wanting, suddenly, for something interesting to happen, to be said, to mark the occasion.

'Oh, you know the kind,' says Torimitsu, blushing.

'I'm not sure I do, I'm afraid. What do you mean?' She pressed on.

'Leave it now,' says her mother.

'What is it, I wonder? What kind of stories could it possibly be?'

Nakamura smiles at her, a boyish, quick smile which darts across his face. Is it a reward for her act of courage? Or is he making fun of her? Does he think her naive, ignorant? Yoko is reminded of the last time he smiled at her. There was a time when he was supposed to marry her, after all, and in exchange for a marriage proposal she received this little splinter of a smile.

* * *

After Yoko's brother married, he left his clothes, his video games, his old computer; he left photograph albums from family holidays and address books; he left the desk-lamp on, his futon sweating in the cupboard, and he left his mother and sister. He moved to the Osaka office, taking his wife and two young boys with him. A month after he left Tokyo, her mother's stomach complaints began in earnest, and Yoko found herself taking her mother to the doctor almost daily. She spent hours counting pills, dividing and labelling them into correct days, consulting doctors and un-medical people alike about her mother's symptoms. The night-time was the worst for the pain. Her mother lay awake, groaning and complaining of being too hot or too cold. She took to sleeping late into the morning, something which she had never done while Yoko's father was still alive.

Yoko's mother began to find walking difficult. Around the house was no problem, but the street on which they lived suddenly stretched for miles and miles. Almost overnight, distances which had been perfectly manageable became unbearable. The world reduced to projections of pain: the walk to the toilet, or the postbox, or the front door. Yoko had a special bath fitted – hot water alleviated the symptoms – and every evening she undressed her mother and helped her onto the special chair which lowered her into the water like a forklift manoeuvering boxes in a warehouse.

On such a night, after Yoko had lifted her mother from the bath, and had begun to pull the trapped hairs from the plughole, her mother said, 'Pass me the photographs, won't you.'

A birthday card for Yoko had arrived from Osaka that morning. Her brother had, rather cruelly she thought, bought a card with the number '36' written on the front. Inside were two photographs of the boys, one in his junior high school uniform, the other still in the anonymous soft clothing of infancy.

Her mother, wrapped in towels, held the photographs with her damp fingertips. 'So much like your father and your brother. The expressions, so haughty!'

Yoko pulled a clump of hair from the plughole and wrapped it in tissue paper.

'It was good of him to remember your birthday.'

Her brother's life was entirely unknown to Yoko; she could only imagine a house exactly like the one she lived in, but filled with running children. The birthday card curled slightly in the heat of the bathroom.

'I want to have children one day,' said Yoko.

She said it without thinking, in the same way you might conjecture about future day-trips. She hadn't meant it as anything but the barest, simplest statement of fact, and yet as soon as the words left her lips, she felt things change around her.

Her mother arranged the towels around her legs, wrapped another towel around her shoulders, hiding as much of her body as she could. Yoko continued to push the last of the bathwater down the plughole.

'Is that so?' Her mother said at last. 'And what will I do when you're busy running a household? We both know I can't... You know I'm in no position to live alone.'

'Don't think anything of it,' said Yoko. 'I don't know why I said it.'

'Your brother and his children. His wife,' she began, 'as things stand I wouldn't be welcome in their house. They don't have the time.'

'I know. I...' Yoko wanted to say Please forget it, but she couldn't bring herself to. It was as if, by saying the words, she had made real a desire she didn't know she had.

Yoko helped her mother into her underwear, gently holding her ankle and guiding it through the leg-holes, the white fabric sagging in the middle.

Torimitsu was an old friend of her mother's from flower arrangement class. They spent the earnest, studious hours dedicated to Japanese art gossiping furtively over New Year bouquets. Torimitsu was not a professional matchmaker, but it was a passion of hers to nurture and sustain a large network of acquaintances made through her husband's family and her inability to be on her own for more than an hour.

'Wouldn't you feel lonely without her? It's not unusual to keep the last one to yourself, no one would blame you. If she doesn't find a good candidate herself then it might be for the best. I can tell you from personal experience,' Torimitsu solemnly advised, 'living on your own is an abhorrent, unnatural condition.'

'Oh no', said Yoko's mother. 'Not at all. What kind of mother would I be to deny her the life she wants? In any case, Yoko and I will live together. We'll have grandchildren together. She's thirty-six', she confided, 'When I was thirty-six I'd had two children already.'

They agreed that the candidate should be older than Yoko, and it didn't matter if he was divorced, although, naturally, an unmarried man would be preferable to a man with history. He should be at least 165 centimetres tall, since, unfortunately, Yoko herself had proved to be a little too tall. He should have a stable income and a job in Tokyo. Yoko would not be open to moving away from her mother, so this was the most important consideration of all. He must not have any plans of moving away in the future, either. Anything else – appearance, interests, personality – all the lesser details and minutiae which accompanies a human being were at Torimitsu's discretion. At the end of the New Year flower arrangement class she already had a candidate in mind. They paid for the flowers, wrapped up the young pine branches, needles and red-buds in newspaper, and said goodbye. Two days later, a formal letter from Torimitsu, addressed to Yoko's mother, announced Nakamura's arrival.

'Isn't it too soon?' ventured Yoko, standing in the doorway.

Her mother sat with her legs outstretched, tights rolled down to her knees, the veins on her legs throbbing.

'Too soon?' replied her mother.

'I feel as though I'm being hurried.'

'Aren't we in a hurry?'

'Who is he? How will you know if I like him?'

Her mother read out the letter. Unmarried at forty-two, but otherwise very appealing: a deputy manager in an automobile firm based in Shimbashi. A lover of traditional arts, fine dining, the theatre.

'That means nothing. What sort of person is he?' pushed Yoko, angry at the coldness of the letter which talked exclusively of Nakamura as if he were a prize horse at a market. There was no mention of Yoko at all.

'You'll find out soon enough,' said her mother.

'It's too soon, really,' said Yoko.

'What are you afraid of?'

'You'll all be watching me,' said Yoko. 'I don't like to be watched.'

'Isn't this what you wanted?' asked her mother. Yoko fell silent. 'This is your chance,' continued her mother. 'This was our agreement. We'll try it once, and if it doesn't work, or he proves disagreeable, then you don't ever have to do it again.'

In the week before the meeting, Yoko worried about her looks and her weight and stopped eating unless her mother insisted on sharing a meal. Yoko was unsure of her appearance; could not imagine her face being singled out for any kind of praise or evidence of beauty.

Gradually, over the years, her appearance had become flattened, emptied of meaning, like a view from a bedroom window which you see every day and which you can no longer describe in terms of beauty or ugliness. But this meeting was calling it all into question – here, in the mirror, she stared at her sloping eyes, the pale skin, the wide mouth revealing a set of off-white teeth. When she spoke or smiled or listened, her face changing into familiar avatars, she couldn't tell whether this or that attitude was more pleasing to the eye.

She occasionally lost courage, complained, and tried to cancel the arrangement entirely. But her mother wouldn't hear of it, not because she particularly looked forward to the meeting, but because she could not refuse Torimitsu's offer of help. Yoko tried to picture this man, this Nakamura. But he was nothing but a blurred outline between two old women.

And yet, despite all her concerns, Yoko longed to be introduced to the world of marriage that seemed to be going on all around her, but which had, until now, passed by her untouched, like a spectator on a bridge watching a river flowing by. Yoko imagined her wedding day: yes, she imagined dresses, and invitation cards, and conjured up scenes from films and edited their scripts to suit her. But the dream which gave her the most pleasure was the one where she sat down with her mother and told her that she was pregnant. And in this scene her mother took her hands in hers with tears of joy in her eyes and all the pain in her limbs, in the pit of her stomach, all of it was lifted away.

In the taxi on the way to the restaurant, Yoko felt sick. 'It's just the nerves,' said her mother. Torimitsu-san was driving, and her mother sat in the passenger seat. Yoko put her hand to her mouth, the other on her stomach. The obi was too tight, wrapped doubly around her waist. Another corner and perhaps she really would be sick. The Tokyo night sky, dotted with electric lights, the unfamiliar buzz of traffic and people scared her – the neighbourhoods she had visited in the day transformed into a foreign country.

'He's a poet, an artist, a lover of the theatre,' said Torimitsu when Yoko finally caught her on the phone the day before. 'You'll get on, I just know it.'

The restaurant was not the traditional venue Yoko had envisaged. It was Western style, but they were shown to a private booth. There were two padded benches and a narrow table, decked with appetisers. Nakamura was already there, waiting with another woman whom Yoko did not recognise, but who turned out to be Torimitsu's sister-in-law. The party was introduced awkwardly, as both Nakamura and the sister-in-law had to slide across the bench to greet the newcomers. It was embarrassing to watch this inelegant shuffling. Yoko saw the condensation on the iced tea, the silver bird pin on the sister-in-law's lapel, the wax sheen on the table. Yoko noticed her mother draw back from the sister-in-law, unimpressed by impolite language, perhaps, or was she nervous too? Torimitsu threw herself into the fray, energised rather than bewildered by this playacting. It was only thanks to her determination to make a good night of it that Yoko finally let her eyeline creep as far as his hands. His hands, folding the hot serviette into a tight square; his sleeves, the buttons of his white shirt. His voice came to her from a distance. She could not really hear him, or take his words to have the same meaning as normal, everyday language. After all this waiting, the trembling excitement, it was too much, too much.

'I've been told that you're a fan of the Kabuki theatre?' he said.

'She is,' said her mother. 'She goes with me every month.'

'Every month? Is this true, Yoko-san?'

She looked at her mother, and her mother nodded encouragement.

'Yes,' Yoko managed. But the word sounded like a foreign language she was hearing for the very first time.

'And what is it about the theatre you enjoy so much?'

'The costumes are splendid, especially at the Kabukiza,' said her mother.

'Certainly. And what about the actors? Do you have any favourites?'

'Hanafu Oku, surely,' continued her mother. 'He is the greatest actor of our generation.'

'Yes,' said Nakamura laughing, 'I see your mother likes the Kabuki. But what about Yoko-san?'

'Yoko doesn't have favourites.'

'Is that so?'

His voice was flat, suddenly lacking in energy. Yoko could not hear if he was angry, desperate, or simply miserable. She still could not bring herself to look at his face. The conversation dwindled, Yoko felt the evening failing, deflating around her. Finally, he excused himself.

'Why don't you say something?' said mother, as soon as he'd left. 'What's the matter?'

'Leave her be, it's only nerves,' said Torimitsu, soothingly. 'You look beautiful in this light. No need to be shy.'

Why was it that Yoko couldn't look at his face? Why was it that with every word he said, every sincere address, she felt herself draw further and further away? Here, the wall behind him, his black shoulders, his hands; these were what captured her attention. And when she spoke, she was sullen. Her mother wrapped her body up in vest and stockings, underbelt and overbelt, braided cord and kimono, obi and haori jacket, but she had forgotten the most important area of all: her face – her mouth and eyes. Wasn't Yoko entitled to protection? She wanted a mask. White paint, a new mouth, downturned and furious, enraged and passionate as if charging into battle; the pointed black eyebrows of an actor and red streaks to hide the shape of her cheeks. She unfurled this mask from her sleeve and blocked out his gaze; she folded it about her and demanded that no one, no one lift it from her face.

'You know Yoko and I are very close,' announced her mother near the end of the meal.

'I see,' said Nakamura.

'I'm not sure if it has been properly communicated to you, but if things were to develop in the way hoped, then, you understand, it's not possible for me to be parted from her.'

'I understand.'

'And if, the things do develop, and children come into

the picture, well, then, I think it should be understood that I, as the oldest member of the household, should be in charge of directing their care, their education and schooling....'

'Shall we ask for water?' said Torimitsu, laughing at nothing. 'I suddenly have a terrifying thirst. It's the hay fever. The pollen is awful this month.'

Parting at the doorway, the two women left Nakamura and Yoko alone for a moment while they settled the bill. It was a minute that Yoko would never forget. Nakamura stepped close and said,

'You must think me old, or past my prime, and perhaps I am, and if you think that then I'm sorry you were made to come here and suffer my company.'

He smiled sadly, almost sheepishly, like a lovesick student. 'In any case,' he went on, 'the photograph doesn't do you credit. I'm sure you could have better men than me.'

Yoko found herself laughing out of confusion. She wasn't sure whether he was insulting her or proposing marriage. He took out a cigarette and put it in his jacket pocket, then he caught her eye and smiled.

Yoko woke early – at five or so – and forced herself to return to a thin sleep, skimming the surface of a dream. A list of chores from her mother, and money to buy clothes, were left on the change dish by the front door. Her mother was still asleep. In the shop, she wandered the aisles, unfolding shirts and summer dresses, holding them against her body, and putting them inexpertly back in their place.

At the end of the day, her mother received a phone call from Torimitsu. Yoko answered it, but the tinny voice on the other end asked for her mother.

'He doesn't want to meet again,' said her mother.

'No,' said Yoko. 'No, of course.'

'He said it seemed that you'd been dragged there against your will. Was it against your will?'

'No, you didn't drag me, mother. I wanted to go.' She suddenly felt terribly tired. 'I think I'll lie down.'

'Wait.'

She held out her hand and grabbed Yoko's wrist. They remained like this: her mother on the tatami mat, Yoko standing over her. 'I hope you're not too disappointed.'

'No.'

'But you can see his point of view.'

Yoko nodded.

'We've tried it now, haven't we?' she said beseechingly. 'You can't say that I was a bad mother to you. I gave you a chance at what you wanted. At that kind of life.'

'Yes, I won't forget,' said Yoko. 'You're good to me.'

Later, in the waiting room at the doctor's surgery, her mother read her magazine while Yoko saw into the future: the narrow world of the doctor's desk, the examination bed, the blue plastic chairs, the printer churning up pills. The nurse helped Yoko's mother onto her feet, and as she made her way to the examination room, her mother paused,

'Yoko,' she said, looking over her shoulder, 'come with me, won't you? I never know what he's saying to me. He talks to fast and uses fancy doctor's words. Come with me.'

***

The bell rings in the theatre. People begin to make their way to their seats. A young woman who Yoko does not know joins them, appearing from behind Nakamura like a child from behind a parent.

'My wife,' he explains. She puts her hand lightly on his arm and withdraws it; her round face peers up at him.

'We'd better go in,' she says to her husband.

The wife is a little fat, with rounded upper arms and stomach pushing the fabric of her pink dress. Her body speaks of comfort, health. Not like Yoko's thinness, disappearing under the Kimono fabric. Her face is round too, with large black eyes, smoothed over with glittery make-up. There is something brash in her attitude. Yoko realises she might know about her and the arranged dinner with Nakamura. The realisation strikes her like a blow: how they must have laughed together! The husband and his new wife, at the idea that he could have married her, a woman barely able to speak, a woman scared of the dark and loud noises. They must laugh about me when they're alone, Yoko thinks, or over dinner with friends. They greet each other perfunctorily: Yoko bows but the wife hardly bends her head. Instead she turns to talk to Torimitsu. As she does so, Yoko realises with a start that she is not fat, but pregnant.

'Have you had much luck?' Nakamura says, as if reading her mind.

'With what?'

'Finding a husband,' he says quietly. Shocked by the

directness, she immediately looks at the floor, blushing. 'I'm sorry. It's rude of me to ask like that. I don't mean to offend.'

'No, no,' she says. 'Please don't worry about it. The truth is I've stopped looking.'

'Then you've found someone.'

She shakes her head.

'I'm interested, but you don't need to tell me, how many have you been on...? I imagine that between your mother and my aunt you must be very busy.'

'Hardly,' she says. He waits for more. 'Actually, there was only one.'

'If that's true,' he says, faltering. 'If that's the case then...' he tries again, but advice eludes him. 'If I may, you shouldn't give up after only one dinner.'

'I'm getting a bit old for it now.'

'Nonsense,' he says.

She looks at him then, openly. His answer is dull and flat like a heavy stone. She sees in his narrow face the blunt and naive expression she often saw in her brother when they were growing up together: it was the expression he'd affect when he tripped into a world he couldn't understand. Walking into the bathroom where Yoko soaked her underwear in the sink, for instance, or when, in rare intimate moments, Yoko's mother complained of sleeping alone. The discomfort of having entered a world he thinks of as female. Averting his eyes, words failing. Now Nakamura is guilty of the same embarrassment. Nonsense, Yoko thinks. It's not really a different world at all. It's just that something is lacking in him, just as it was lacking in her brother.

They take their seats. The Nakamuras sit two rows ahead, the wife's head resting on his shoulder.

'A terrible woman,' whispers her mother.

Yoko smiles, 'it's alright.'

The theatre is full. All along the sloping stalls, the audience members cross and uncross their legs, open and shut programmes. The lights dim.

'You were right, I suppose,' says her mother, 'it is better in the evening. More lively.'

She pats Yoko's arm, because of the suspense, the excitement of the first act. The curtains rise and a hush spreads across the audience. Her mother tenses.

There. Someone enters at the dark hidden space behind the runway. Yoko feels his presence. And then the musicians take up an ancient beat, hitting the stage floor with wooden slats. Hanafu accedes to the stage for the last time, soft white footsteps pattering from another world. His face hidden by a fan; his secrets untold.

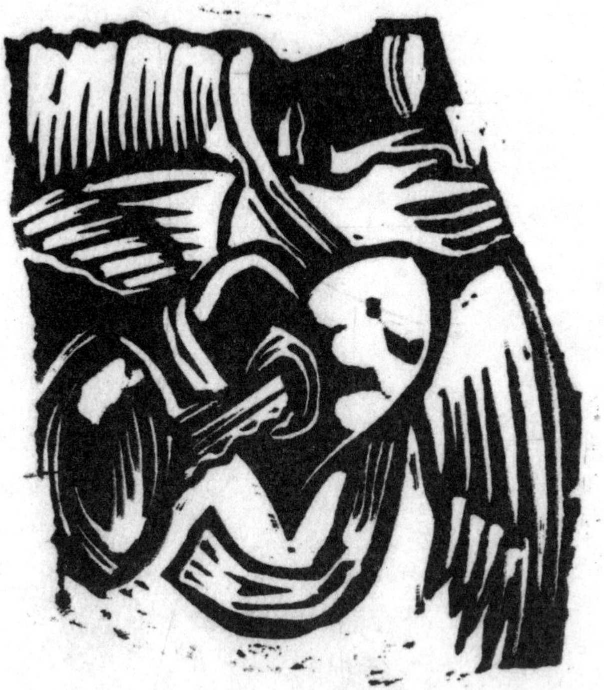

Keeper

Rebbecca Ray

There is nothing unusual about the vehicle, except that its clock reads 000,005, which is unusual. She raises and casts back the garage door, revealing it without a flourish.

'Why don't you drive it?' the woman says.

The man steps between the boxes of VHS tapes and the garden wheelbarrow uninvited. He crouches down to look beneath the wheel arches. He leans in towards the passenger window, shading his eyes with nested hands.

She answers, 'I didn't want it to devalue.'

'But you've never driven it.' The woman doesn't come any nearer, either to the garage or to her. She has a blood red faux crocodile skin handbag hanging from one of her folded arms. She thinks Helen is trying to take them for a ride, but that's the last thing Helen wants.

'It's a long story,' Helen says to the woman.

The man asks for the keys.

The advert specifically states *only five miles on the clock* and this brings a fair welter of calls. Everyone is looking for a good deal – for reliability, Helen thinks. But no one likes a deal that's too good to be true. Every call she receives also harbours suspicions. As many days arrive on which new people come to view it, nights go by when the vehicle remains in the garage.

He opens the door, this man, who has come with a wide-brimmed white hat, which is easily more ostentatious than his partner's bag, and which he is now forced to remove. He is casual, but he's excited Helen sees. He surveys the unmarked interior, the upholstery, each thread of which lies in parity with the next. The vehicle has not simply been valeted.

He leans inside and deliberately displays no care in the way that he takes the front seat. He allows himself to put his hands at 'ten' and 'two'. She watches him start the engine. It starts without impediment, beginning to issue nitrogen and water vapour and carbon monoxide into the farthest quarter of the garage.

He leaves the seat. The woman looks at her own feet and at the currently empty road and the Audi they came in. At the rear of the vehicle, he presses his boot over the exhaust and releases it, over it, and releases it. His boots are Timberland and bear no relation whatsoever to the hat he is still holding. He ceases to do this and allows the exhaust smoke to once again rise around his shins.

As much as Helen dislikes the woman, without any rationale really, she is touched by a wave of fondness for the man. He is just shy of middle age and starting to run to fat, dressed smartly but in a way that speaks of effort, and he stands there attempting to pretend he doesn't want the vehicle more than he can presently remember wanting anything.

'So what's your price?' he says.

The woman with the red handbag looks on calmly from the pavement outside.

'Make me an offer,' Helen suggests to him.

'Well I don't know, what ballpark are you looking for?'

'I really couldn't say. You tell me. Make me an offer,' she responds.

She sees his gaze skim back across the bodywork.

'You must have a price in mind,' he says.

So Helen asks him, 'What do you think it's worth?'

The words always produce the same reaction – or perhaps it's the way she says them. They're not even aware they're doing it but gently, Helen sees, both of them recoil from the vehicle, its gleaming lines no longer candid, its darkened windows treacherous.

She only advertises in the classifieds and only the ones where she need not list the price. She would have had to choose on eBay. She would have had to choose in *Auto Trader*. Only in the backs of the local papers can she find a place to list the sale without needing to state what it's worth.

She doesn't know what it's worth, that's the truth. Or why it's not worth exactly the same as it was when he carefully performed the three point turn that parked it where it stands now. She keeps it ticking over.

Where does it lose value? In the dust sown across the paintwork? Through the soft dark stain of exhaust across the concrete floor? If someone can tell her from where the value seeps, and at what rate, then she'll be able to tell them exactly what it's worth now.

She remembers how they sat there as he killed the ignition, his hand resting on the gear stick, the garage door open before them, showing a breadth of suburban, homely road. And the sound created by adjusting one's position on the seat, and the smell of the carpets – untouched by any other shoe. Her bag and his coat on the backseat behind them. His smile beneath the shadow of the garage roof.

Still the man wants it. He wants it despite the fact that he no longer trusts his own desire. But his wife now, his partner, she's crossed her own internal line. Nothing valuable ever comes at the buyer's price.

Helen watches her walk the herringbone brick driveway for the first time and step over the threshold into the garage. She does this in order to justify her change of mind, though she's not aware of why she does it. Helen knows her type only too well.

She says, 'I think if you expect to sell it, you need to be prepared to explain to people why it is you've never driven it yourself.'

Helen recalls the stockbroker's wife who'd stood approximately where this woman's standing now, younger, prettier, darker-haired, possessor of zero faux anythings, and how she'd come to the edge of the doorway, putting one hand out to assess the vehicle through her index fingertip, having performed every other test of which she'd been advised.

'I don't expect to sell it necessarily,' she answers quietly.

She doesn't want to admit to this woman – least of all a woman like this, and in front of this nice-seeming man – that she can't drive.

He told her he would take her to the beach, a beach that he knew well but that he hadn't seen himself for years, and they'd swap seats and she could jump and stall and lurch all she liked on the safe expanse of sand. They'd look up the time of year when low tide and twilight coincided.

He said he'd buy her weekly lessons. It was nothing, he said, by comparison – he knew that, but nonetheless they'd be a gift from him. He said a large number of things that did not turn out to be true and she remembers every one of them she can.

She has been tempted to try to make it out to that beach herself, not to drive of course, but to walk there.

It's the name she can't remember. Regardless of the way she tries to retain things, some of them still seem to slip from her grasp.

Perhaps one day she'd still like to drive. Perhaps one day she'll still take lessons. It isn't as if his absence makes her incapable. Every third night she runs the vehicle to keep its engine working – sits for a while in the shadowed driver's seat herself. And she thinks about forward movement, and she listens to the sounds of the new seats, the upholstery, smells the smell of this thing that could have been his. And she understands what it feels like to want to drive away somewhere. What it must be like to be this great big four by four, staring blind in the dusty dark morning after morning, at the indistinct lines of light around the garage door.

They didn't travel far and so it's not long until they're home. At seven they eat. At nine they retire to the bedroom. He takes the left hand side of the bed, she takes the right. She can't sleep without adopting this arrangement.

They don't sleep yet of course, though with each year that passes they seem to do so at an earlier time. She lies beside him on the covers in her nightdress and the dark blue dressing gown that he bought for her, with sweeping kimono sleeves. Not a choice on his part, but a request on hers.

'I don't think the woman had her feet on the ground,' she resumes. 'If you ask me it was laughable. I mean what sort of person tries to sell a car like that? Or puts an advert in the paper when they don't even want to sell it *necessarily*? Maybe that's how she gets people to visit. She's desperate for company.'

He doesn't answer her.

He takes his book from the night table but in fact he doesn't want to read and he gazes at the changing pictures on the tv screen.

She says, 'How much do you think she paid for it? She obviously got it new. It must be more than twenty grand's worth in that garage. Well someone's bound to think it's a deal I suppose. Maybe someone who's good with mechanics. Can things go wrong on a car that's only driven five miles? It looked perfect. She obviously keeps it in running order. But I'm glad you didn't want the thing. I don't think I'd have wanted to get inside.'

'There wasn't anything wrong with it,' he says.

He regrets this though, because she begins to speak again. She talks about the smell of the vehicle. She talks about the way the woman watched him. 'She liked you,' she says. 'I could tell.' But in all the things she turns back and forth as she keeps talking, trying to exorcise this other woman – who he can tell she feels has in some way won – at no point does she ask him what figure he might have thought of offering. Or if he considered making the vehicle his at all.

He is himself under the bedcovers; newly changed bedcovers scented with the fabric softener she prefers. Numbers travel through his imagination: miniscule, exotic numbers. He holds his book. He looks at the tv screen.

The central heating is on its rounds again. It's hot already, surely hotter than it's meant to be – he turned down the thermostat only a week ago. But he can hear the water now, working its blunt head down the pipes, first from the kitchen where they're painted olive green, then through to the bedroom here, where they become cream like the vine-patterned paper, and thence into the radiators – already distended, scalding – fixed to every wall but the one against which his head now lies.

Disneyland

Richard Owain Roberts

Happy new year, Robert. We are very grateful for your hard work over the course of the last year, this effort did not go unnoticed. We feel this great relationship can go on from strength to strength. We have carefully selected seven hundred tasks for you to complete over the course of this year and are sure they will be completed to the best possible standard, setting a fantastic precedent for the rest of the year! Yours faithfully.

Robert closes his laptop and looks at his iPhone. The clock reads 4.30 a.m. Robert thinks,

This is fantastic news.

Robert walks into the bedroom. His wife, Eva, is asleep. Eva is snoring. Eva quit her job as a social worker six months ago and in the last six months has,

a new tattoo (owl)
read Richard Yates (the novel)
read Richard Yates (the writer)
a new tattoo (cat on a bicycle)
improved her core strength via the pull-up bar (monkeying technique)

Eva deleted her Facebook two months ago and told Robert that every day is the best possible excuse to feel good about living.

Robert looks at Eva and puts his hands on his head. Robert closes his eyes for a moment and forgets that he is standing up; his legs buckle a little before his regains his balance and opens his eyes. It is dark outside, and windy. The windows rattle a little. Robert thinks,

This sound is okay, I should record this sound.

Robert picks up his iPhone and stretches his arm out towards the window, recording.

Robert leaves the bedroom and walks downstairs and into the kitchen. Robert and Eva live in west Wales. The house they live in was described by the estate agent as needing 'complete modernisation throughout'. When they looked round the house for the first time, Eva said that all of her dreams were coming true in realtime. The estate agent asked Eva what she meant by the term 'realtime'. Eva looked at the estate agent and said, 'Will they accept the asking price?'

Robert and Eva moved into the house with their cat,

Abw, and a bullmastiff puppy called Moses. The animals have contrasting personalities but get along nicely. Robert told Eva that he finds most people's personalities leave him numb. Eva told Robert that she finds most people's personalities leave her disappointed. Eva sometimes talks about how she perceives herself to be an unpopular person. Robert tells Eva, 'It's you that doesn't like them.'

They paid four hundred thousand pounds for the house and this meant they had eight hundred pounds left over to complete renovation work. The house is made up of,

a hallway which leads off to,

a large living room that has an open fireplace at either end
a small snug
a large, square kitchen that has original floor tiling dating back to the late nineteenth century

the staircase is old and creaks, it leads up towards,

a large bedroom
a large bedroom
a small bedroom
a bathroom
a small bedroom.

All of Robert and Eva's furniture and possessions from their old house fit inside the large living room. On their first day in the new house, Robert and Eva ate a packet of plain wholemeal wraps at 8 p.m. Eva said, 'This is the first time in a new place that we haven't ordered Domino's on the first night.' Robert said, 'Domino's hell lifestyle.'

Robert sits down at the kitchen table and runs both his hands up and down the tabletop. The table was a gift from his mother; it cost five hundred pounds at auction. The table is old and beautiful and won't ever break. Robert eats two Weetabix with soya milk from a brown tapas bowl. It is very quiet in the kitchen. Moses is asleep. Robert's iPhone vibrates.

Dear Robert, please can you confirm receipt of our last email to you, dated January fourth, 4 a.m. This is so we know you understand the forthcoming schedule of tasks. Yours faithfully.

Robert puts the iPhone down and runs both hands up and down the tabletop. Robert is unable to lift his hands. He needs to lift his hands from the tabletop to be able to stand up. Standing up is an essential first step towards returning to the small bedroom. Once in the small bedroom, Robert will be able to contact his employer to confirm that he is making a start on his task. The first task of the year. January the fourth, 4.30 a.m.

Eva walks into the small bedroom and says, 'What are you doing?' Robert turns and looks at Eva; she is wearing grey tracksuit bottoms. Robert says, 'I'm editing footage and then putting it back together again.

Sometimes the footage has to be at a slower speed, or sometimes it has to be looped, or sometimes it has to be in negative. I'm not sure if this is what editing is, I think it's what they want.'

Eva stretches her arms above her head and clasps her hands together momentarily. Eva says, 'How long have you been up?' Robert says, 'Three hours.' Eva walks towards Robert and kisses him on his forehead. Robert rests his head on Eva's shoulder. Eva picks up a T-shirt from the floor and puts it on. The T-shirt has 'N. W. A.' written on the front in large black lettering. Eva says, 'If Eazy-E was still alive it would be a good reality show for him to live in west Wales, maybe something to do with canoes or abseiling. No?' Robert nods his head and presses cmd+v on the keyboard. He presses cmd+v four times in succession which makes four, three second, identical clips. Robert presses cmd+o and selects to slow the first clip down by ten percent. Robert presses cmd+o and selects to slow the second clip down by twenty percent. Robert presses cmd+o and selects to slow the third clip down by sixty percent. Robert looks at the screen and shuts his eyes. Eva puts her hands on Robert's shoulder and squeezes a blackhead.

* * *

June the fifteenth, Robert and Eva look at Facebook.

'Imagine being with someone who thought it was appropriate to put photos of food on here. Am I a bad person?'

'No. Is food worse than rhetorical question statuses?'

'Yes. No. What will you write if I die?'

'I'll write. I don't know, um. *Eternal sleep, with no conscious thought, my body burnt and scattered in a humanist ceremony? Don't mind if I do!* then update your profile picture with a Cambodian skull.'

'Lol.'

'If anyone writes anything underneath, I'll write, *who are you* or *you're next* or *it can death.*'

'Lol.'

'Someone from my PGCE deleted me.'

'Lol, cold.'

'She had Asperger's, or she said she had Asperger's.'

'Message her and ask why.'

'Okay.'

* * *

Moses is now nine months old; it is August the nineteenth. Most mornings Moses and Robert walk and run together through the woods beyond the bottom of the back garden. To get there they walk through two fields, a small unkempt apple orchard, and another field.

Robert stops walking and breaks a dead branch from a tree and holds it in front of his face like a sword. Moses circles Robert and jumps up and down, barking. 'Your bark sounds funny when you jump, Moses.' Robert looks beyond the branch and sees a man looking back at him. The man, a farmer maybe, has a gun resting on his shoulder.

'Hello.'
'You can't be here, this is private land.'

'I didn't realise, sorry. Is it your land?'

'No, I look after it. You can't be here, it's privately owned.'

'Okay. I don't know, it just doesn't seem like it's a problem me being here.'

The man takes his gun and points it towards Moses and says, 'That dog.'

Robert sighs. He is wearing a grey T-shirt and yellow shorts. He can feel sweat running down his back; his heart is beating very quickly.

'Moses, Moses, Moses,' Robert puts Moses on his lead and they turn and walk.

They walk quickly through the field and once they reach the orchard Robert stops and lets Moses off his lead. Robert picks a rotting apple, shouts Fucker, then throws the apple back in the direction of the woods. Robert says, 'Moses Moses Moses.'

Robert and Moses run without pause until they arrive at the gate at the bottom of the garden.

* * *

Eva is in the garden with Abw and Moses. Abw is lying on a piece of rotting wood and Moses is rolling in a puddle. Eva says, 'You guys, what are you doing?' Eva looks at the outbuilding and shouts, 'We should turn this into a space for guests, we should turn this into a space for guests.'

'Where?'

'The outbuilding.'

'Okay.'

Eva picks up a tennis ball and throws it up in the air. She looks up and loses sight of the ball in the sun. She thinks,

I don't know.

Eva walks over to the pond to see some tadpoles. Eva looks at her reflection in the water and shouts, 'Am I still a babe, am I still a babe, am I still a babe?'

'Yes, more so.'

***

The house being exposed to the elements means there is constant upkeep required to ensure comfortable and tidy living. It is November.

Robert and Eva climb a ladder and sit on the roof so they can replace broken and damaged slate.

Eva looks at her hands and smiles. Her eyes look more Asian than they do on most days. Eva points towards the clouds and the sun and then towards a bird, a heron.

'Heron.'

'Heron. Heron flow from the eighties. Heron and heron. That's a homophone.'

Robert puts his hands on the collar of his T-shirt and pulls down. He stops pulling and lets his hands hang from the collar. He looks at the heron.

'When I was eight I went to Disneyland, Florida. Jim and I were waiting to get served food at one of the stalls. Jim started talking to the man in front of us in the queue. Eazy-E. The man was Eric Wright. Eric Wright. Eazy-E from N. W. A.! Eric Wright! They talked and then Eric Wright said, What up nigga, want a photo. Jim said, Thank you, I'm a fan. Jim said, This is my little brother, Robert. Eazy-E said, Young buck, nice to meet you. I wrapped my arms around Jim's leg and pressed my face into his thigh and Jim and Eric Wright, Eazy-E, laughed. Eric Wright, Eric Wright's girlfriend, Jim and I stood and smiled and we had our picture taken. Eric Wright and Eric Wright's girlfriend took their food order and left. Jim looked at me and asked me if I knew who Eric Wright was, who Eazy-E was. I started crying because I recognised him but didn't know his name. I felt humiliated, but Jim said it was okay. Jim said, They took the photo on their camera, that's funny, that's a really funny thing to happen.'

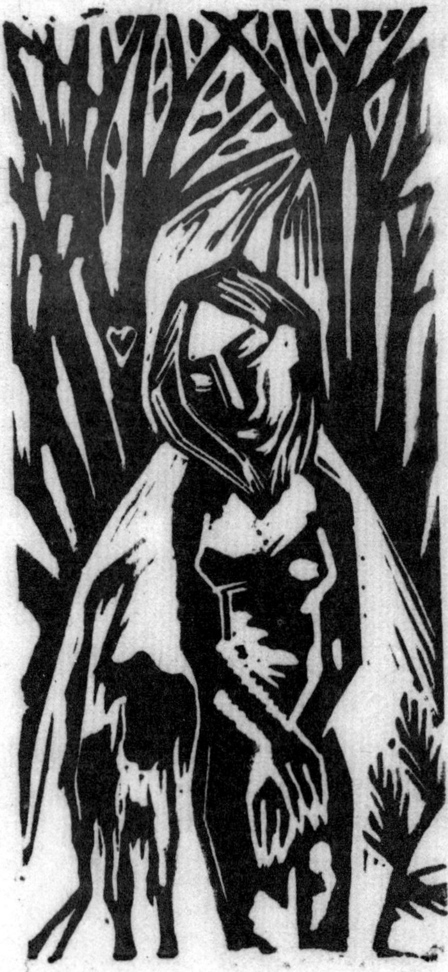

Into The Inwood

Rhian Edwards

The air was crackling in the woods that morning. It was as if I was surrounded by a swarm of gramophones, their stuttering needles scouring helplessly for another song. Or maybe I was in the heart of a forest bonfire, the charring twigs clicking their fingers like the warring gangs in *West Side Story*. Either way, it was an ominous static and it was sweeping through the undergrowth like a wild boar.

'There's at least a rape and a murder here every year,' you said, the day you introduced me to the place. 'Never walk here at night or without the dog'. And with that, this became my daily ritual and excuse for doing very little else. At least by dragging the dog along, I wasn't being entirely useless to you.

The cinnamon pathway helter-skeltered up the hill. Black iron streetlamps manned the margins, the lantern glass smashed on each passing light, prison guards turning a blind eye. A lightning-blasted tree stood sore-thumbishly in the middle of the spiralling trail. It looked more like a flasher on the brink of spreadeagling its raincoat than a shrub scarred by an act of God. I peered inside the hollow of the trunk, expecting to find a sandwich wrapped in a gingham napkin or a grey squirrel playing solitaire.

Empty dime bags littered the forest steps like autumn leaves. I wondered what drugs they had contained. I imagined the dealer going to the stationery shop to buy his weekly roll of narcotic coin bags. Was the woman behind the counter suspicious? Was she in on it? I rewound his day and pictured him cobbling together his shopping list on a Post-it note from the same stationers. I envisioned an inventory of Methamphetamine paraphernalia in addition to yoghurt, Pringles and pomegranate juice. I was rather impressed by his ability to multitask. Clearly the drugs had not got the better of him; after all, he did have a business to run.

It was while I was congratulating the fictitious dealer that I heard the crackling. I looked to the labrador for answers. Judging from her wild abandon as she massaged herself in a mattress of ferns and fox piss, her canine sixth sense was clearly taking a sabbatical. How could she gambol in the foliage at a time like this? Why wasn't she growling? Why weren't her nostrils hoovering the forest floor like a bloodhound?

I kept looking behind myself. Not because I perceived any human threat, a mugger, a rapist or worse a jogger. It was the woods itself I didn't trust. It seemed the indigenous topiary was playing Grandmother's Footsteps with me, inching ever closer while my back was turned, playing statues the instant I dared to look. Or maybe the vegetation just looked uncannily like its earlier self.

I started to suspect the whole place was booby-trapped, hard-wired with Wile E. Coyote, ACME-manufactured snares. Aggressive plant-life was camouflaged as benevolent shrubs, designed to inflict acute dermatological damage that no oatmeal bath could cure, metamorphosing its victims into *Batman* villains. Or worse, the entire ecosystem thrived on the blood of hapless wanderers, siren-singing us into a quicksand of seemingly innocuous mud, condemning us to become part of the Inwood soil forever.

Once the dog and I had ascended the crack den steps, we made the steep descent into the bowels of the wood. Scrolls of stinging nettles hedged us in, giant coils of the stuff, mangled at the sides of the path like trench barbed wire. Some of the nettle cobs had unravelled their elongated limbs and stretched out to touch us like adoring fans or connived to tap us on the shoulder before delivering a knuckle sandwich, pumped to the brim with formic acid and histamine.

And then there were the creeping nettles, ninja nettles, crawling on their bellies across the trail, razor-sharp and lethal, Shogun-trained to tripwire you or shred your soles to ribbons. And not a dock leaf in sight.

We were in the basin of the woods now, caged by tulip trees and red oaks. A rug of wildflowers, downy yellow violets, bloodroot and Dutchman's breeches spread out before us, as did a maze of crisscrossing footpaths. It was disorientating and there were acres of it. I contemplated scratching crosses onto trees with the tennis ball chucker, using Hansel and Gretel tactics to get my bearings. I looked to the dog for her internal compass. She cocked her head and scratched herself.

I was now on my guard for the next instalment of herbaceous threat and the dog was nowhere to be seen. There was the small matter of the ivy and the oak with the word 'poison' prefixing them like a panic-mongering, tabloid headline. Back home, ivy was a Christmas decoration, a quaint blanket to the facade of the house. And the mighty oak was the muse of watercolours, a shade for merchant ivory picnics, a Pagan totem for worshipping and shagging. Never did the ivy or oak come with an incandescent sticker bearing skull and crossbones.

'Leaves of three, leave it be,' was the nursery rhyme mantra you drilled into me. Even the convivial clover had been blacklisted. In fact everything verdant was under suspicion. There I was combing the forest floor for vindictive fauna in a witch-hunt of McCarthy proportions. Maybe this was how everything in America survived and flourished; by having a serrated edge, a spiky attitude, telling the world not to fuck with it by fucking with it first. Maybe it was the surrounding vegetation mainlining the dope from the dime bags, thorns evolved into makeshift hypodermic needles.

This was the real urban jungle, a streetwise treescape, shrubs on drugs. And none of that Meow Meow shit either. Hell, they had even found a way of palming off plant fertilizer onto the human drug market while muscling into our own stash.

It's only a matter of time, I thought, before we will bear witness to a gangster triffid draped over the top of the Empire State Building, a crack-whore blonde screaming in its branched fist. And the whole world will be glued to its Boob tubes, while the monstrous fuchsia climbs the tip of the Empire needle, to prick itself with the ultimate hit, the miasma of the Manhattan skyline.

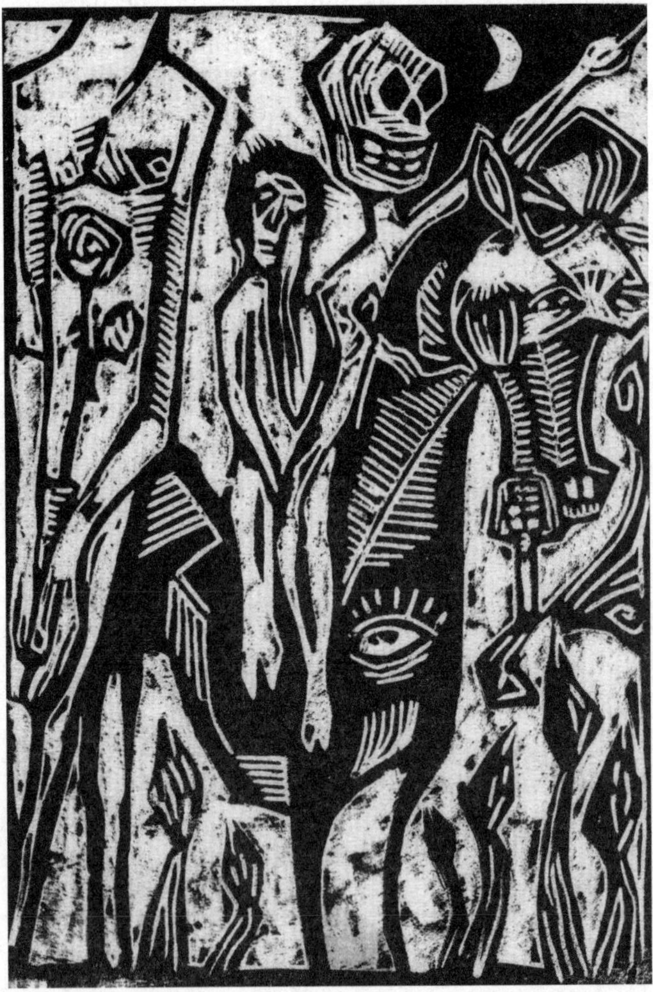

Moles

*Monique Schwitter
Tranlated by Eluned Gramich*

He sits on the edge of the bed in his underpants, fanning himself. His dark brown hands dance in front of his fair chest, which he so despises, and which he hides away from the daylight and from strangers' eyes, under his shirt. He's drawn the heavy acrylic curtains, wiping out the white sunspots on the mattress, and switched on the bed-lamp. His gaze passes over the telephone on the bedside table. He falls back on the mattress and reaches for the book again.

'Like every evening, Bovet stood in the open doorway and looked out into the darkness. He breathed in deeply, closed his hands like a funnel over his mouth and hurled his revulsion into the surrounding loneliness: *Just stay away! Keep off!* He thought of Solange as he locked the door for the night, and smiled inwardly. The plump spinster had, in his memory, remained graceful and elfine, just as he'd imagined her as a little boy. *Arthur,* he heard Solange's voice and saw her cradle the huge pillow in her arms, *off to bed!'*

He forces himself to read it slowly, word for word, restraining his eagerness; the words droning in his hot head.

Arthur! Keep away! Shoo!

He dozes off, dreaming of Solange and her huge pillow. She looks like his mother in the dream; she shakes the pillow and out come millions of moles. She smiles fairylike, *here is your life's story*, she calls to him and blows a kiss and waves goodbye.

He wakes up, the lamplight blinding him; his head lies heavily on the book. He turns to the phone.

He picks up the receiver and waits for the dial tone, and puts it down immediately, considers whether he should call the reception and have the chambermaid come up with a bottle of water or a coffee or both and decides against it.

He turns the tap on, bends and drinks. He holds his head under the water and hears ringing. Does he hear ringing? He turns the tap off jerkily and listens. Water runs into his eyes. The phone stays mute.

He writes his initials in the front of the book with a ballpoint pen, without thinking. Then he looks at the two letters and shakes his head.

He found the book in the hotel corridor, on the maid's cleaning trolley. He heard her hoovering in the next room and, giving in to a sudden impulse, he pulled the book out of the trolley's rubbish compartment, disappeared with it into his room and wiped his hands briefly on a towel.

He leafs through the book and can't find the place where he'd fallen asleep any more. The book has been well-read. The rough, porous paper is stained and swollen; the spine criss-crossed with folds, and squished mosquitoes lie buried in between the pages. His powerful dark fingers rummage through the pages; his eyes fly over the lines.

He tries to remember. He stopped with the fairy and the moles. Where the old, lonely Arthur Bovet thinks of Solange – his father's woman – who told him as a child that moles represent a life's story. Solange claimed that he who has many moles can expect an exciting, wild, rich life. She claimed a fairy came in the night and shook a huge pillowcase, scattering the moles.

Now he remembers exactly. He just read the part where, for Arthur, the fairy always looked like Solange. For Arthur Bovet, the narrator and the character melted into one being, until now. Yes, that's where he stopped.

He hears footsteps in the corridor. He puts on a shirt and opens the door. The chambermaid brings fresh towels. He blames her for interrupting his reading. *When else*, she says, *you haven't left the room once. You watched me make the bed and fluff up the pillows. You saw it*. He takes the towels from her and slams the door shut. *You never leave the room anyway*, calls the chambermaid through the door.

He fetches the journeyman's cloth from the wardrobe, in which he has carefully packed his gear – jacket, vest, bell-bottoms, collarless shirt, broad-rimmed hat, journeyman's cravat, handkerchief, shoes and woodturned walking stick. He places the cloth on the mattress and packs his bundle. Wash things, underwear, shirts, tools. He attaches the tied-up bundle to the yardstick and is satisfied.

Hey, you, I'm ready, he says belligerently to the telephone. *Dear God, South Africa, do you hear me? Nor Aarhus, Granada or Dubai, but Cape Town. I don't want to learn Spanish, Danish or Arabic, but English, because I can already speak it a little,* **do you hear?** He glares at the phone.

He leafs through the book, looks through it and thinks, I already know all that: how the young man arrives at Bovet's out-of-the-way farm; how Bovet says, *the roof's leaking* as the boy enters the room; how the boy answers, *I'll repair your roof in exchange for bed and breakfast*; how the older man says, *if you like* and goes to bed; how he lies there, the old Bovet, for the rest of the story, he won't get up anymore; he'll undress, lie down and think about his own death; how he wants to think about it, but instead he'll think about his life again, which remains a mystery to him, arbitrary and lacking a central thread, even in hindsight.

I already know all that, he thinks, but he's not sure if he's read it or not.

He stands in the shower and rinses himself with cold water, the nipples of his hated chest hardening. They disgust him. He tries to listen out for the sound of ringing while in the shower, through the thundering stream of water.

He lies wet in his bed and counts the moles. By 117 he has the feeling they've multiplied overnight or, he thinks, the fairy has struck again in the unguarded nights. He who has many moles can expect an exciting, wild, rich life, he thinks, and looks at the phone.

He calls the reception and orders a coffee. Then he opens the book randomly and reads.

'The young man looked for a place to sleep and something to eat. He decided on a room next to the stables, in which stood a bed and a chair. A picture on the wall, small curtains, nothing else. He found an open carton of milk and a chunk of hacked mutton in the fridge. The boy poured himself a glass of milk and spat out the first mouthful. The milk tasted of blood, of goat and stable. He decided to start repairing the leaking roof, even though he had no idea what to do and had learnt nothing.'

He pauses and sniggers contemptuously. *Layabout,* he hisses. He then follows the eager-to-please young man of the book as he hopelessly attempts to fix the roof. Because of this failure, he forgets the telephone, forgets to talk to God, even forgets the heat.

A knock. He raises his head. He places his forefinger as a bookmark between the pages, turns on his side and gets up as quietly as possible, the book in hand, the finger jammed. He stands beside the bed and stares at the dark green carpet. Another knock. The door opens. *I'm naked*, he says without looking up. He hears the surprise in his voice. The door closes again. Silence. *Mr Roeder, your order.* The voice of the chambermaid. He hurries into the bathroom with the book in hand, stands behind the door and calls, *Yes!* The maid enters. *Sorry*, she says, and *here you go*. He hears her put the tray on the bedside table. He sticks his head round the door. *I'm sorry*, he says hoarsely.

He hasn't touched the coffee. He stares at the tray, the cup and the milk jug for a while before reading on again.

'The young man sat for hours at the old man's bedside and watched him. *What do you really want? Why don't you carry on? You've got your whole life ahead of you*, argues Bovet from time to time. The boy continues to watch him. *You've been lucky here*, he says suddenly and points out a mole on Bovet's arm. He gently pulls the covers away from the older man. *Here, look, that was the beginning. You should have kept to the north-west, directly towards this big mole*, he drives his finger at the mole on his collarbone, *but possibly your compass was lacking. You journeyed south: a mistake that almost everyone makes in a crisis. Everyone always thinks their instinct says south, yet south is mostly wrong.* The old man drew the covers up. *Get out. Just get out and leave me in peace, finally, peace. Leave me*, he shouted, bitterly regretting that he had, in a sentimental moment, told the boy of Solange, the fairy and the pillow.'

He dips his forefinger in the cold coffee and licks it off. *Yuck*. He skims the next 20 pages, because at the same time he's considering complaining to the maid about the cold coffee. Then he laughs at the idea, shakes it out of his head, and dives back into the story.

'Bovet lay on his stomach and let himself be washed. The boy wrung the sponge out, put it away and trailed his fingertip down the old man's back. The water drops hung on his wrinkled skin like little magnifying glasses. *Can you paint by numbers*, asked the boy, *you connect them, from number to number, and make a picture*. He laughed. *Only, the moles don't have any numbers, so it's not easy to find a path, back and forth, and recognize the picture: a bird.'*

He reaches for the handset and dials the number of the reception. Not to complain, no, only to ask for the maid to come again. He hasn't thought of an excuse. *Read to me*, he thinks he could say. *Read my moles. I'd like to know what lies before me, what I can expect.* When he hears the concierge's voice, he puts the phone down.

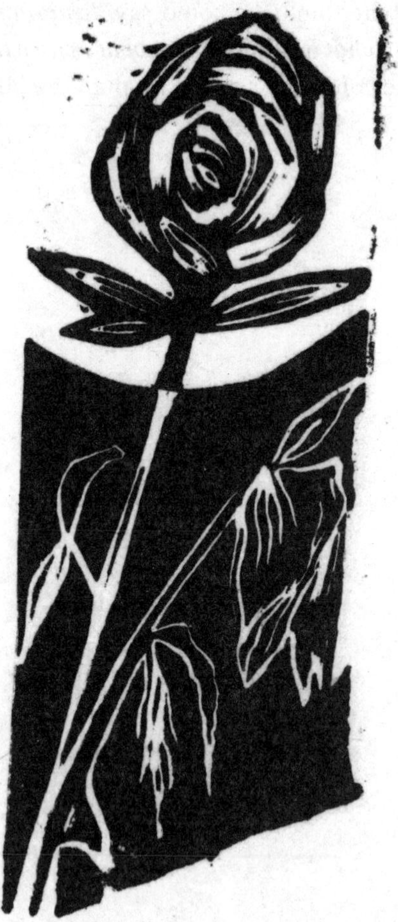

Soft but Definite

Sarah Coles

I know about grown-ups having secrets. It's something to do with the smell of them and their big fingers. They give each other a look sometimes that they think we don't notice, but we do, and we store those looks up and use them like an alphabet. There's something about these grown-up secrets that makes them sad – all of them – even the happy ones with clean fingernails, like Miss Tyler. I know that, because one playtime, she was standing in the yard, just looking at the floor a little way in front of her. I'd wanted to hold the bell and had to call her name three times before she even noticed I was there.

Jane has secrets. That's my grandmother but I'm not allowed to call her Granny or Gran because it makes her feel old. She's not even old. She's only sixteen years older than my mother was. I live with Jane because I killed my mother. Jane didn't tell me that. No-one did –

I just used the alphabet of grown-up looks to find it out for myself. She used to tell people that my mother had gone outside to put my bike away when it'd started raining, to stop it from rusting up even more, and she'd slipped and fallen down hard, hitting her breast on the step. That's what gave her the cancer that killed her. Whenever she got to the part about it being *my* bike, she'd give a look to the person she was telling, who would, in turn, give her a similar look. Then they'd look at me. I'd pretend not to notice but it was as easy as spelling out the word B-I-K-E.

But Jane has secrets besides that one, which I can't quite read yet. I think grown-up secrets are something to do with their hairiness and their flesh. I saw Jane naked once, when she was getting changed. Her tummy was in rolls that rested on top of each other and her skin was like the outside of a grapefruit. She screamed when she saw me, like I was a terrifying thing, like a spider.

My father left when Jane was pregnant with Zach. So Zach is kind of my brother and my uncle, which is weird when you think about it. That's another thing I worked out from the alphabet. I don't really think about it much because mostly he's just Zach. I'm not supposed to mention it anyway.

I always think that the words 'secret' and 'shame' go together. They don't rhyme, I know, but their meanings sort of rhyme. We have these workbooks at school that say things like, 'Snail is to shell as bird is to ____' and you have to write the word 'nest' in the space. 'Bird is to nest as secret is to shame.' Or shame is to secret – either way.

I remember the first time I really, properly understood the word 'shame'. I must have been about six because Jane was still pregnant. Things were tight at home. That's what Jane used to say – tight. So tight that we'd have the heating cut off every now and then, because Jane couldn't afford to pay the bill. That meant we'd have no hot water for washing ourselves, or our clothes. Jane hit on an idea though. She'd scrabble together enough coppers for us to go to the swimming baths. She'd put some of our dirty laundry in the bag with my bathers so that she could wash it in the showers with shampoo. If we didn't have any shampoo, we'd borrow some that people had left lying around. Jane never came in swimming with me but she'd check on me now and then through the glass of the 'viewing gallery'. You had to be eight to go in swimming without a grown-up but I've always been tall for my age so nobody thought to ask. I remember my bathers stinking a bit from the dirty laundry, and they were too small and went up my bum but I'd soon forget that when I got in the water.

Nobody taught me to swim. I'm a natural. We have swimming lessons at school now I'm in Year 5, so I've learnt some proper strokes since then, but at the time I'd just bob about and doggy-paddle around. I'd make a point of not looking at the viewing gallery window so that I couldn't see Jane calling me to come out. One day, though, I'd been in the pool for ages. I was getting hungry and the ends of my fingers were starting to pucker like pink raisins. My fingernails were white around the edges and looked like tiny moons. I kept looking at the window but I couldn't see Jane at all. I decided to go and find her.

I paddled through the cold, shallow footbath that led to the changing room and showers but Jane wasn't there. My clothes were folded on the bench and my towel hung from a peg. I dried myself off quickly but the towel wasn't exactly fresh and after I'd put my clothes back on, I was just as grubby as I'd been before my swim, except now I smelled of chlorine on top of it all. I saw one of my socks from the laundry in a pool of water on the floor by the door that led out. It was a stripy one from my favourite pair. I squeezed it out, rolled it into my towel and went out into the foyer.

Jane was there and three men were talking to her. Well, one man was talking to her and the other two were standing with their arms folded. The one that was talking to her had a shirt and tie on. Jane's sleeves were all wet and she was holding a binbag that was dripping onto the carpet of the foyer. Jane was quiet. One of the men went and pointed to a sign on the front door which said 'No Itinerants'. From what I could hear, somebody had told the swimming pool attendants that there was a gypo washing her clothes in the showers. I heard the man who was pointing to the sign asking Jane if she was illiterate. I know what that means. It means you can't read. Jane can't read all that well, actually but that doesn't mean she's stupid. Just like being poor doesn't make her a gypo. I knew all of that but it didn't stop me feeling the shame I just told you about.

What happened that day made me feel two different kinds of shame. That had been the first, but the second kind of shame was even worse. I had been so embarrassed and ashamed of Jane standing there, being called a gypo, dripping on the carpet – her huge stomach sticking out and her sleeves all wet – that I sneaked past, went out of the door marked 'No Itinerants' and walked all the way home by myself. I sat on the doorstep for nearly an hour until Jane came back, lugging the binbag that held the wet washing. She didn't say anything about it and we had beans on toast with grated cheese on top for tea. After that, I felt the second sort of shame – the worse kind. I had a heavy feeling in my stomach and a kind of dragging behind my eyes for leaving her there, dripping and being called a gypo. I should have stuck up for her or at least stood by her – helped her carry the bag. After all – she is looking after me after I killed her daughter. I went to bed early that night and I cried quite a lot, even though I didn't really believe that falling over could give a person cancer.

I had a secret until recently. My secret was that I would sometimes play with Ben Gates who lives with his father by the railway track. Ben Gates is about twenty-three but he has this thing that keeps him like a kid, and he talks as though he's only just learned to speak English. Jamie Jones says that Ben's father makes him wear a nappy at night but I think he's just being horrible. My secret was a secret for two reasons. One, because I wasn't allowed to play by the railway track, which was fair enough, and two because I wasn't allowed to play with Ben Gates. I couldn't understand why Jane would be like that about Ben. You'd think that people who are used to having a rough deal would be kind to other people who are having a rough deal but that's not always the case. I liked playing with Ben because he knew all the best places for finding birds' nests and lizards and frogspawn and hundreds of other things that I would never have seen on my own. I don't know how he knew all of these things – all of the names and the habits of these creatures – he never went to proper school. I suppose he's just a natural, like I am at swimming.

One evening, when it was just starting to get dark, he took me and Jamie to this secret place on the other side of the railway track, where there's an old tunnel that's been sealed off. Ben was getting pretty excited as we pushed through the brambles and he was giggling and telling us to hush. When we got there, he froze, put a finger to his lips and with the other finger, he pointed to the top of the sealed off tunnel where there was a gap, about a foot square. We stood there for what seemed ages and Jamie was getting impatient and starting to fool around, when we heard this soft sound – soft but definite – like a hundred blown leaves against a window. Then, from out of the dark square, as quick as heartbeats, twenty, forty, I don't know how many small, dark shapes came pulsing out into the evening air. Bats. Ben's mouth opened into a big grin. We watched them whirl and dive and they came so close to our heads that we could feel the wind of their flight but they never once hit us and they never once missed the small entrance to their tunnel, in spite of their speed. Ben was making all sorts of noises, and laughing and biting his fist. When I went to bed that night, I had a feeling in my stomach that felt like diving into water. I had wanted to tell Jane but I'd have got into serious trouble. It was a secret that didn't feel like shame though.

Not long after that, Ben was sent away for showing his cock to Laura Duggan. She'd screamed all the way home and couldn't go to school for a week. Later, I found out that *cock* is just a rude word for *winkie*. I couldn't understand how a winkie could be a frightening thing. I've seen Zach's lots of times and it's just a funny thing – a bit of extra, wiggly flesh. Nor could I understand how the word *cock* is rude and the word *winkie* is okay, when they both mean exactly the same thing. Jane says I'll understand all of that when I'm grown up.

I'm doing well at school and the teachers like me a lot. Especially Miss Tyler. They seem to be amazed by all the things I can do even though my marks aren't really all that much better than anyone else's. I think they're surprised that someone who's poor can also be brainy. I could have told them that ages ago.

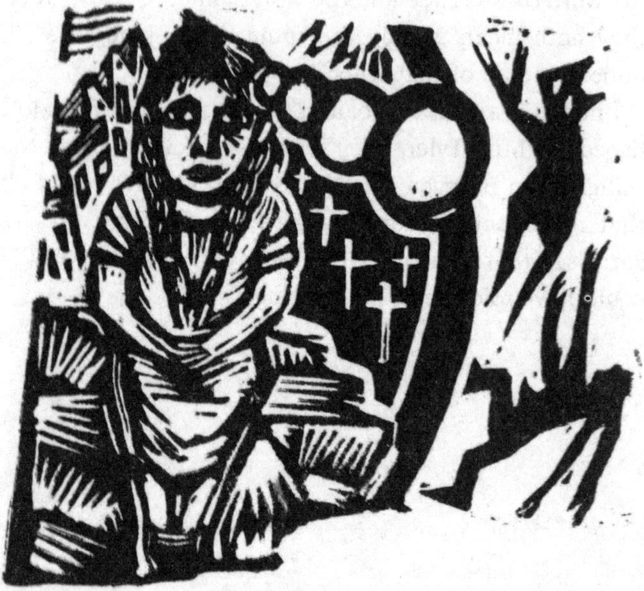

On Dry Land

Peter Krištúfek
Translated by John Minahane

I'd been seeking that peace for a very long time.

The peace where *the soul wearied with the contests of life* at least for a moment finds rest. The graveyard exhales the coarse scent of grass and May flowers, some of them fading on the tombstones, but many more are already pushing through the undergrowth, which will soon need mowing. Even though words like *graveyard*, *peace*, *soul* or *rest* might incline more towards the dead than the living, as far as I know and assuming that everything isn't a delusion, I still have the corporeal fluids flowing in a live body and the nerve fibres are still vital and sending out information and disinformation.

I tread from foot to foot on the cracked asphalt pavement.

The graveyard scarcely gives the impression of a monument from the mid-17th century. The wise comrades of the 1970s, manically intolerant of history, completely altered its shape (in line with cadre principles, they were mainly the offspring of clay- or oil-smeared workers who had barely learned to read in the previous generation – a fine example of socialist genetic engineering). Out of the blue, a notice appeared then on the gate, demanding that the two-hundred-year-old skeletons should kindly gather up their limbs and take their gravestones on their backs and go off to blazes somewhere else. The monuments roughly flung on the grass patches today give the impression of someone having carelessly let them fall from his pocket. Of course, many persuasive reasons were found for replacing the historic wall with a concrete eyesore. I've got obviously erroneous ideas about beauty, and I've grown accustomed to that. The excesses of architects in today's satellite suburbs evoke similar feelings of horror in me, but that's not my agenda. Any opinions I have ordinarily differ from the views of the majority. The foot you're standing on is mine, thanks for asking.

I've come here to seek peace.

I'm standing by a venerable tombstone, barbarically clasped in grey concrete by two rusty hooks. Whoever put those things there and was satisfied with his work (did he step back, narrow his eyes, and contentedly smile...?!) must have been a complete idiot. The inscription tells of a Hungarian countess, garlanded with first names, surnames and titles, who had gone off to France to pine away and die, at the age of forty, after the fatal accident of her twenty-year-old son in February of an incredibly distant year.

That year too had a February; interesting.

Fat mosquitoes are taking cover from the sun in the bushes, and an intuition of my blood draws them forth from their daily watch. This too is an indication that I am alive, and I feel relief. Sometimes it's harder to believe that, for example, on some such languid sunny day near the end of May when time, charged with responsibilities, suddenly became empty and waste and left me washed up on dry land. Though I'm not gasping for breath, not that, no. I'm making the best of it.

Otherwise, to be truthful, I regularly spend days forever up to my neck in the dessicating concrete of my customs and habitual rituals – which admittedly give me support and hold my life together, but like the iron construction serving to ensure that a person doesn't fall from the balcony, they gradually become a grille of solid bars and in the last instance take away my freedom.

A bloody smudge on my calf compels me to walk on further.

I disturb a flock of pigeons. They are different from the ones that nest above our bathroom. More peaceful, solemn, slower, with white collars round their throats. I've seen them already in another graveyard. That's how the messengers of souls might look, the *psychopompoi*. Immediately they fly off. Evidently they have figured out that for some time to come I will not be part of the classical inventory in a place like this, and so there is no need to give me a premature escort. Flagstones, bones, candles and gilded inscriptions… mushrooms, blackbirds and functionaries in overalls… tears, quiet music in a very rounded and mournful register, spilling out here from a nearby church. It sounds like a blob of purple chewing gum stuck on the cardiac muscle.

There will be time for that yet.

I sit on a bench and read a book I've got with me.

Strolling near me is a young woman with a moderately desperate expression, pushing a quiet pram. Again, after a while a man in a suit passes by me, a manager, who has come here to eat his miserable sandwich, while giving his colleagues the impression he has lunch in a fancier restaurant than the one they go to. Life is eternal pretence that we're something we aren't. I've an intimate knowledge of that. There's no end of examples in these surroundings. Even those old photos on the gravestones! Beautiful young faces that apparently departed at the peak of life, although they were over eighty and had rheumatism, lumbago, angina pectoris, or severe diabetes.

Some of the statues and adornments have been stolen by visitors, who took them for a collection or their private hoards of bizarre things.

One of those 'tram-bugs' from my childhood is walking along the retouched black-and-white cheek of a bulky girl. We used to slaughter them by hundreds in the sandpits, but still they're everywhere: nature obviously makes provision for the wastage caused by young human beings.

A small branch is lying on the tomb of the Haluz (Twigge) family.

A gentleman with a mighty moustache and a harsh, wild gaze is called Sztarenka.

Also lying here is Tido Gašpar, who for safety's sake is not mentioned on the worn plaque announcing where the graves of important personalities are to be found. Following the war he received a life sentence but was released after thirteen years. For a moment I call up the image of that face marked by alcohol, nicotine, and other vices besides. I imagine him somewhere in the 1920s, puffed-up, full of strength, happy and awash with the sap of life. Perhaps some people live more intensively than others. Like, say, Carl Jetting, a traveller of the century just folded away, when there was still something to discover, an adventurer with a spectacular barque on his tombstone. The past is plainly only a thought. I imagine him sitting on the toilet, but that doesn't work. He always wore showy clothes, and he wouldn't sit down for anything on earth!

I follow the young mother who is slowly pushing her pram under those trees with the strangely cut leaves, which I can't identify; the manager in the suit contentedly chews the last juiceless bite and faces the decision whether to throw the greasy paper under a bench or into the nearby rubbish bin. The functionary in overalls tells a joke and involuntarily spits on a two-hundred-year-old tomb: after all, he's at work and the dead are only common extras in his straightforward, uncomplicated life.

A small particle of the fractal.

A fractal is, according to theory, an irregular fragmented geometrical shape, of which each part is a reduced copy of the complete figure. And so just as basic human groups exist, in all places in our world one can find *human fractals* who copy them. I often amuse myself by observing this phenomenon. Every graveyard has a young woman with a pram, who looks a bit desperate, and a functionary in soiled overalls, cynical and dull-witted; equally, one can find there an eccentric like me, who just sits and for inexplicable reasons gapes at what's around him. Just as every tower block has a coarse and domineering woman acting as tenants' representative, a harassed irritable malcontent with a claret-coloured face, whose anger never quite finally makes him die of a heart attack, and an introvert trying not to catch anyone's eye, opening his mailbox with a pounding heart... The Mandelbrot quantity in every street. The Koch snowflake with repeating persons in its structure.

All of that exists before our eyes.

The world is an equation.

I don't know, perhaps I casually dozed off, but time unexpectedly took a leap, as sometimes happens. I imagine it as a girl with plaits, walking slowly along the street, then she races after a cat and leaps over a puddle, sits on a stone verge and daydreams, quickly gets up and vanishes suddenly round a corner. The graveyard is a place where adults come to play. Here they build their own castles of sand and marble, with baking moulds and little shovels.

With vertebrae and skulls.

The sun is low, glimmering through the crowns of the plane trees and elms, and throwing crooked stains on the pavements. I feel a languor and pleasant fatigue from the fresh air, from the hardy greenery rolling in from all sides. Such a condition must either be suppressed or enhanced. How pleasant it would be to sit here with a bottle of wine and drink it on the bench in the thickening twilight, at the end of an anonymous day somewhere amidst the week!

And now I rise, stroll across the road and in the nearby supermarket impatiently reach for bottles, then put them back on the shelves, until finally I decide on one. Mentally I praise the felicitous brainwave of modern winemakers, who have shown a profound understanding of open-air drinkers and also think lovingly of those absent-minded persons who left the corkscrew at home.

At the checkout I observe the crowd of people beaten down by daily routine, smelling of sweat and cares. Further human fractals. The skinny teenager with headphones on his ears, despising everyone; the stocky fifty-year-old woman radiating garlic; the fed-up assistant in a costume which that morning was still uncreased; the loony talking to himself and his beloved plastic bottle. Fat faces and sparse hair, each with an idea of his own dignity or importance.

Civilisation, I reflect, has brought us all that, and immediately I yearn for the society of my patient dead, who no longer either suffer or complain. About taxes, children, weather, problems, friends and enemies. About all the others. About politics and illness. Who do not waste time drinking beer in some stinking smoke-befugged hole or beside the television. The current age breeds profound frustration. It's complicated, when from all sides you hear: *You're a personality!* or *You count for something!* – but it's not so, because people are not equal. They divide into those who are more and less frustrated. And the first lot want to take swipes at the second. The more talented, more capable, cleverer. Hungry beasts stamp on the heads of those who have eaten. And food means *success*. That substantial bit of meat, that blessed carcass, that plateful of soup. Every movement evokes a counter-movement.

I look around me and I have a bad taste in my mouth. A muscular sportsman in sunglasses, smelling of cheap deodorant, presses in upon me from behind: he is so doggedly playing the hard man that he begins to give the impression of an attitudinising schoolgirl. Movement and counter-movement. We are only animals: humbly I accept this fact and I find it rather funny.

Ugh! At long last I'm out!

The graveyard is an oasis amidst the city. I hear the regular hum of the motorway behind the wall. After screwing off the cap I pour the acrid red liquid into my mouth, and its taste changes suddenly to smoke and blackcurrants: the French for blackcurrants is *cassis* and it seems to me I'm pronouncing the word as I swallow. *Ca. Si. Ca-si... Casi.* This wine was made on the other side of the planet (if the label can be credited), somewhere beneath the Chilean Andes, and the makers had no idea where it would be drunk or by whom. Llama droppings, moist wind from the Pacific, sweat, dust, blood, air currents. And suddenly, unpronounceable and unimaginable Europe. Squeezed too far to the north, too far to the east. After all, Siberia to us is only an empty plateau. Beautiful! The weary little man in a vineyard on another continent has no idea of the city in the middle of which I'm sitting.

And why would he?

He couldn't even pronounce the name without stammering.

The bottle is empty. The large mosquitoes by now have ventured to leave the shade of the dark green cypresses, and they're whistling and stinging. The functionary in a soiled T-shirt is impatiently treading on a thuja; his sweat comes to me on the breeze. The gate closes behind me, grating. Blackbirds cry and mate high above the earth.

A bit of molten black dropping falls on my shoulder, looking like a windfall from the poisonous berries that grow on the other side of the graveyard. I wipe it off with a tissue.

The young woman with the pram flees down the pebble-strewn path, not wanting to spend the night with the dead.

Profound peace, alone the entire day. The first star can be seen in the sky diffused through the leaves of the trees. It twinkles dimly.

I cross the road and head homewards.

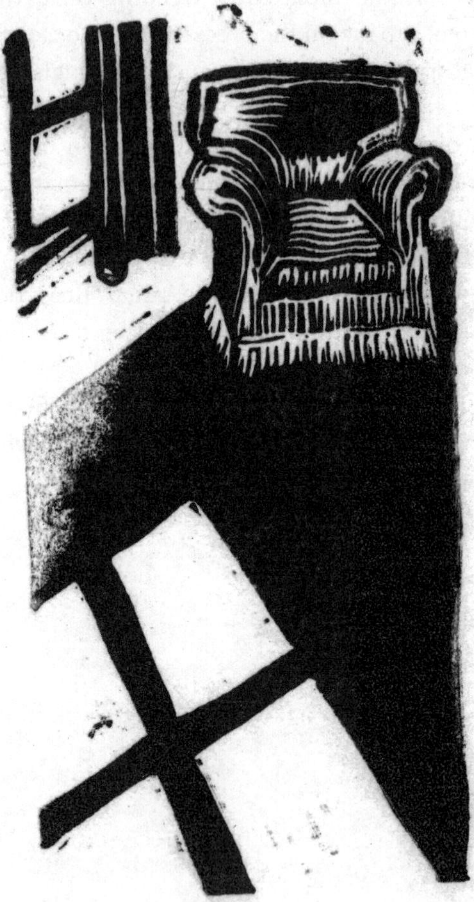

Friday

Carly Holmes

I swear they just moved again. The hills. When I turn my head they shift and tremble in my peripheral vision, then flatten themselves once more against the horizon. Mauve and grey and blue.

But there's so much less horizon now, so much less blue.

The phone rings, and rings again. She lays down the smart skirt and blouse she'd been holding against her body, spreads them gently across the bed and grimaces at her mirror's reflection. The journey down to the hallway and the impatient telephone takes longer with each passing month. Each step a careful evaluation of risk. The phone has stopped again, started again, before she reaches it. She eases herself down onto the chair and scoops up the receiver.

'Mrs Ford? I've been phoning and phoning... I wanted to make sure you're okay. Mrs Ford?'

The carpet is so worn beneath her feet. Decades of heels and toes absent-mindedly tracing the subdued swirls of colour, while the bodies and the hearts attached to those heels and toes ache and hope and break. She should probably hire one of those carpet-shampooing machines; give it a good clean while she can still bend a little.

'Mrs Ford? Are you there? It's Sammy, just wanting to know that you're okay.'

'Please, Sammy, just call me Penny. You make me feel so old! Will you do that for me, please?'

She laughs at his hesitation and imagines the sound squeezing its way through the phone lines, arriving damply at his ear. He laughs too.

'Okay, sure. I'll try, anyway. Are you all right though? Is there anything you need?'

Luka appears from the kitchen, spine curving right and left as she wags her tail. It's nearly time for lunch. She screws up her eyes with love and wonder, sighs loudly, and then stretches and shimmies back to her basket.

'Mrs Ford? Penny? So, is there?'

'Sorry, Sammy, is there what?'

'Anything you need? Anything I can do? I worry about you, alone up there. Do you want me to bring over some groceries or collect anything? Do you have everything sorted for Friday?'

If she leans forward so that her collarbone nudges queasily against the wooden arm of the chair, she can just make out Luka's back legs pedalling furiously as she chews on the rim of her basket. Attention seeker.

She tries to refocus on the conversation. 'Sorry? Friday?'

Embarrassment thickens his voice. 'Isn't it? I'm so sorry, I must have...'

'Oh, yes! Friday. Sorry, I'm a bit distracted at the moment and Luka needs feeding. No, I'm fine, really. You're such a good neighbour; Geoff would have really appreciated it. Thank you so much for caring, but there's nothing I need. I'm going to be fine.'

There's a spot on the carpet, about the size and shape of a ten pence piece, worn so much thinner than the rest. Is that the place where decades of toes dug in for a second, curled and rigid, as legs jerked with shock or grief above them? Maybe she shouldn't give it a shampoo after all. Maybe she should disconnect the phone instead. Or write a letter to the phone company with a request for compensation. 'Bad news ruined my carpet. Photo attached. I hold you responsible.'

'So I'll see you at the service on Friday then, Sammy, and thanks again. I'd better go. Luka's pestering me for her food.'

Her list is waiting on the kitchen table and she admires the neat columns of words, the precise lines carving them through. Only a few tasks left and they're easy ones. Confirm flowers. Confirm car. Take smart navy skirt for dry cleaning. Try to locate that silly photo of her and Geoff taken at their nephew David's hog roast last June. Bake, and bake, and bake. That can all wait until Luka has been out for her afternoon amble.

When I look directly at them, look them right in the eye so to speak, there is the merest hint of movement subdued, of breath held. And then I look away again and they gasp their relief into the air. Wind rushing past me, around me, through me. And then they shuffle a bit closer.

Penny draws her curtains far too early and turns the radio on. Light seeps around the edges of the material and mocks her quaint old-lady routines. Only another couple of hours to go until bedtime and she can punctuate that wait with a cup of tea, maybe a small glass of brandy, and a final quick walk. She turns the radio off and sits. The phone rings.

'Oh, David! How lovely to hear from you. How are you, darling?'

Luka catches her eye and crinkles her muzzle. Her tail beats slow delight on the kitchen floor. Penny winks, listens, and speaks.

'Oh, don't worry about me, I'm fine. Keeping busy. Will you have time to visit before Friday?'

The worn patch, the particularly worn patch, fits beneath the ball of her big toe perfectly, as if it had been deliberately scooped out to cup the rough flesh. It feels soft as kitten fur against her bare skin.

'Oh, that's okay. I perfectly understand darling. I hope you're not overdoing things, though, you're always so busy... I know, I know, I just worry about you. Okay, I'll see you on Friday. Take good care my darling, and please give my love to Julia.'

In the bedroom she finds a box of photographs and chuckles her way through them until she locates the one she needs. She crosses through another task and then adds a few words to her list: Get photo blown up and framed. There's bound to be somebody in town who'll know where to go for that. She glances at her watch and is cheered by the time. Back downstairs she tips a small amount of brandy into a tumbler, considers for a moment, pours some more. She grins across at Luka and raises a finger to her lips.

In the front room she pats the back of the armchair in apology as she passes it, smoothing the fringe. Sorry, old friend. She sits on the sofa awkwardly, settling and resettling into the slumped curves that have been shaped, over the years, to hold the contours of a body bigger than hers. She twists and wriggles for a while and then gets up, moving back to the armchair and tutting with resigned frustration when it hugs her close, fabric shifting easily around her. She sips and reads and pretends not to notice when Luka slides in, eyes and stomach pinned to the ground, and slithers onto the sofa. Hers now.

When Penny goes up to bed her cheekbones are pleasantly numb and she thinks she may be able to sleep. She lies for a while in the darkness and plans the next day, remembering and forgetting chores, remembering again. She thinks about getting up and adding to her ever-growing list but decides against it. She looks at the tiny twin bulges of her feet beneath the covers, the flat expanse around them, and then after a while shuts her eyes.

On Sunday I tripped and fell when I was walking with Luka. I lay stretched on the ground for a while and the earth murmured beneath my cheek. It was a gentle sound, a sleepy sound, and it made me nostalgic for the time when I used to take joy from this landscape. When we used to take joy from it. I curled up and listened, and didn't move until Luka barked and pawed at me, hungry for her dinner.

When I opened my eyes and stood up, the hills jostled with each other once more to see who would reach me first. I knew then that I had been careless. With my eyes closed, with the heather prickly as a woollen jumper and warm as flesh against my mouth, I forgot to fear them. I forgot that the jumper is now in a bag by the front door with all his other clothes. But the forgetting isn't worth the remembering. They're closer now than ever before.

Penny has completed another three of her tasks before breakfast. She hums her way through her tea and toast and washes up before she can give herself a chance to make excuses. She pauses in the act of removing her rubber gloves to stare at the delicate march of china across her draining board and the morning freezes around her. A teacup. A saucer. A plate. A tableau of widowhood. She passes a hand across her eyes and turns away.

The drive into town usually takes a few minutes, but today she decides to saunter her way down through the valley in low gear. The windows are open and she can smell the warming heather. Luka sits in the newly adopted front passenger seat, watching the scenery spool past, and Penny watches Luka. She hopes to borrow some of that absence of strain and urgency, to just enjoy the ride. She transfers her gaze to the view and notices the rubbish that has collected along the verge nearest to her, counts with shocked wonder the number of drink cans that splash colour amongst the grass in place of flowers. The bodies of the dead animals, the gaudy smear of their fur and flesh staining the tarmac. She wonders if these blemishes have always been there, and if she was just too blinkered, too comfortable, before now to see. Happiness breeds complacency, her mother always used to say.

When Penny reaches town she parks outside the baker's and tells Luka to stay. She winds the windows partially up, checks that the list is in her bag and gets out of the car. First chore; return the bulky parcel of unswallowed tablets to the chemist. She enters the dim coolness of the shop and waits her turn in the queue, spilling loud, bright words onto the polished floorboards in response to the concern and the questions. Oh, I'm fine, really. You know me, I'm a coper by nature. And it was a relief by the end. Yes, Friday. We hope, I hope, you can make it.

She goes into shops, and leaves shops, and pauses in the street a few times to take her pen in her hand with triumph and cross through tasks completed. She waves at Luka, now in the driving seat and craning to keep her in sight.

'Don't worry darling, not long now. I'm nearly finished.'

As she frowns over her list she fidgets under the weight of the sun on her back. The pavement feels suddenly sticky, her shoes too thin, and she looks up at the encircling hills then walks quickly into the gloom of the nearest shop, emerging after a while with her smile repainted and a monstrous hat in pink and black, which she places on her head as she continues with her chores.

She bumps into an old friend outside the post office and allows her chin to drift downwards for a few moments, her shoulders to slump forwards over her heart. As they embrace she settles her bags onto the ground beside her.

'Only three more days, and there's still so much to do. I'm keeping that busy, you wouldn't believe.'

Her friend tugs her close and tips the hat back so that she can look into Penny's face. She doesn't let her go. Penny leans forward suddenly, urgently. She whispers.

'The hills. Have you noticed anything different about them? They just seem so... close.'

The two women study each other for a moment.

'They're watching me, Brenda. Waiting.'

'Waiting for what, Penny?'

'For me to forget about them.'

The friend rears her head back a little way, the better to focus.

'And what will they do when you've forgotten about them?'

Luka barks from her seat in the car. Penny flinches and steps back, smiling.

'Oh, don't take any notice of me. I'm tired, that's all. But only another three days, and then I'll have all the time in the world to relax and get some rest. I sound like such an old woman. You really shouldn't pander to me.'

She laughs and moves away, slipping out from the grip on her shoulders. Marching towards her car, she waves and calls a goodbye. The hat casts a deformed shadow at her side.

The sun has bowed its head and slunk away now. It's cowering behind the bulk of the hills and no matter how high I climb I can't reach it. The half-light it's left behind, this unnatural eclipse, spills eerie patterns onto the heath. Shadows drip and scuttle, and night-time animals haunt the midday gloom, moaning their bewilderment. Luka pesters me to let her out. She longs to chase them but I'm terrified of losing her too. The hills would crush her the moment she took her eye from them.

'That's it! There's nothing left to do.' Penny crosses through the final item on her list and flicks the pen across the table. Luka blinks into the silence and doesn't raise her head.

'Nothing left to do. Nothing.' Her voice is weak and thin in the still, stale air of the kitchen. She clears her throat and tries again.

'Nothing. All gone. I have nothing.'

She pushes back her chair and leaves the table, tries to distract herself by enticing Luka from her bed. Luka turns away.

'Oh, come on, sweet girl, don't sulk. We can play ball up and down the stairs, what do you say? Work up an appetite for dinner.'

She dips and slides towards Luka's cupboard like a pantomime villain, opening it and producing the promised ball with theatrical gasp and flourish. Luka closes her eyes.

'Oh, Luka, please. We've just got today and tomorrow to get through. And we can get through it together, can't we? Say goodbye. Then afterwards we can go away for a while, somewhere flat, and get some air. And when we come back everything will be where it should be, where it used to be, and we'll be able to go for walks again.'

She waits for a second then puts the ball away and leaves the room. Just looking at the stairs exhausts her so she sits in the gloom of the hallway and stares at the phone. Sits and waits.

When it rings she is startled from sleep and thrashes blindly around for a moment. There's no sound at first but the wind and she moans with panic, is about to replace the receiver when her nephew speaks. 'Aunty Penny?'

'Oh, David? David, how lovely to hear from you again. Is everything okay?'

'Everything's fine, Penny. We won't be able to stay over though, on Friday, sorry. But how are you?'

She laughs and strokes the phone cord.

'Oh, keeping busy, you know. So much to do. I've barely got time to sit down these days.'

'You sounded in a bit of a state when you picked up. Are you sure you're coping?'

'Did I? No, I didn't. I was just asleep that's all. The phone ringing gave me a bit of a shock.'

There is silence from them both for a moment. When David speaks again his voice is spiky with concern. 'Look, are you sure you're okay? Do you want to come back with us afterwards, for a while. For a week or so.'

She grins as broadly as she can. The action froths her

words as they leave her mouth, stretching and lifting her vowels. She sounds cheerful and light.

'Oh, you don't have to worry about me. Honestly, David, you're very good but I'm planning to go away as soon as this is all over. I'll take Luka somewhere nice for a little break.'

'Oh, the dog! I'd forgotten about him. He wouldn't be able to come I'm afraid. Julia's allergies. But maybe a neighbour could take it? Or a dog's home. You know, a holiday home thingy?'

'Oh, no, I couldn't do that to her, she'd think I'd just abandoned her. No, David, thank you for the thought, darling, but I'll be fine. It would be nice if you could come for lunch on Friday, give us some time together before the service. I've hired a black limo by the way, it's very posh.'

His response is muffled by the shove of the wind under the eaves and she has to ask him to repeat it.

'That sounds great, Aunty Penny. I'll give you a ring before we set out.'

'Absolutely, darling. So that's settled then. See you on Friday.'

The broken connection growls in her ear, but she doesn't have the energy to lean forward and replace the receiver in its cradle.

I sit at my window and keep watch. I refuse to surrender to sleep. They're crowding around my little cottage now, shuffling closer with each blink, each lapse of concentration. They'll crush me if they can. But I just need to get to Friday. I have to get through till then.

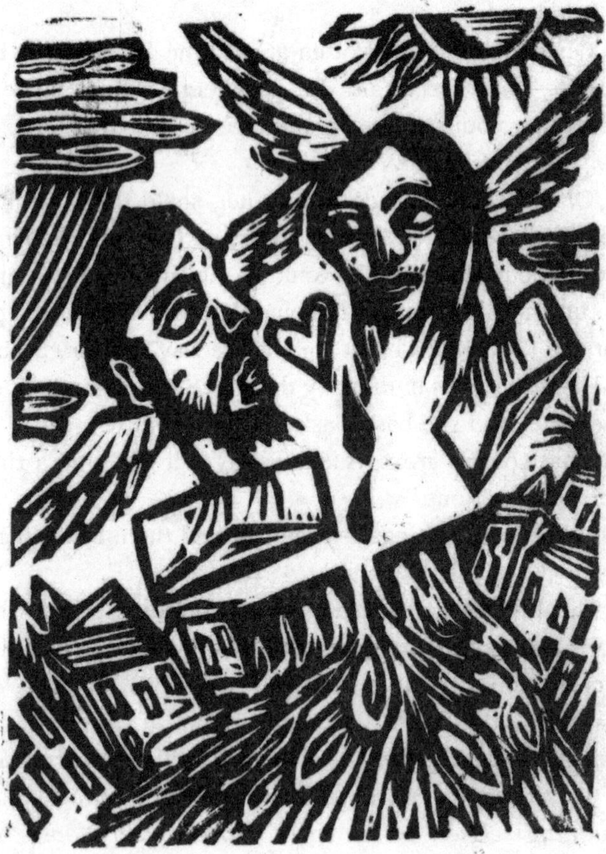

Letters Home

Susmita Bhattacharya

2nd January 2005

My dear Asma,
Salaam-alekum. I reach Cardiff all safe and sound, and start working also. The plane journey so terrible. Seat so tiny and they not show nice Hindi film. Old flop film. No Amitabh Bachchan no Shah Rukh Khan. I waste my money on this plane. Nizambhai go last year in British Airways, and see latest film, *Ab Tak Chhappan*. Remember we see this in Paradise Talkies, just after marriage? Food was so-so. Cold rice and daal. Hard hard chana masala. Chicken like cricket ball.

I am in Cardiff now. Very fine city. By bus three hours from Heathrow. Sorry, by coach. Bus, coach all same things. When you come to UK you also learn many new English words like me. So I practise to write English with you every letter, okay? You practise reading and talking loud. That is good, we get British citizenship fast. Muyazzumbhai waiting for me at bus-stop. Here bus-stop is so big and not crowded. I do not have to push to get into bus or out. Everyone stand in line. In queue. But one thing not good about Cardiff. I find out soon. It is raining raining all the time. Small small drops, like mist. Not like in Dhaka, big fat rain that fall like stones. And so cold, I cannot say how much. My bones feel like *kulfi*. I think I am inside a fridge. So freezing and misty and dark. Muyazzumbhai bring for me a big, black coat. It is very warm. Once I'm inside this coat, I like Cardiff again!

I am sharing big house with three men. Two Bengalis and one from Syria. We all work in Muyazzumbhai's restaurant. Is very big and famous restaurant fifteen minutes walk from house. Royal Bengal Cuisine. But there is no Bengali food. Something called curry. Nothing like home food. All food here called curry this and curry that. I so confused. I learning to make chicken tikka masala and doner kebabs. But I assistant, so I not cooking food in restaurant. Just cutting and chopping now. I cooking at home only. Abdul Mia says I making better kebabs than head chef. But that is secret, as we not wanting to lose job. I go to English school in the morning. Very nice school. People from all countries. One Bengali lady in my class, but she very British. She not talking to me. My teacher, her name is Betty. Her hair more golden than your bangles.

How are you? Hope all is fine at home. Ammi is good to you? You taking care of yourself. Soon you come here when baby is born.

I write again soon,
Hassan.

My name is Hassan Sadikur. I come from Bangladesh. I live in Cardiff. I am married. What about you?

10th February 2005

Dear wife,

I got your letter. But rain falling on it and I cannot read very well. Next time write with ball point pen, not pencil. Happy New Year to you. Don't worry, Betty teacher is old. She married and has big son. She not pretty like you, but her hair is golden.

Our house very beautiful. In UK, it is called terraced house. Many many many houses stand in one line. Long queue. All looking same. One night I coming home and not finding my house. I standing on the road and looking. All same – same colour, same curtains, same doors. I getting very scared. I lost in this new country, this long street with same houses. I don't know anyone to ask. I ask one lady in the street. But she scared more than me. She say something I not understanding and she run inside one house. She close the door bang in front of me. In my area, most people not speak English. I think so. More Bengali. But this lady – what she speak, I not understand.

Then I remember, all houses have a number. This door with scared lady inside has 29 on it. My door is 119. My house in UK. Muyazzumbhai says it is 5101 miles away from Dhaka. But everyday I smell Bangladeshi cooking smell coming from next house and I close my eyes. Then Dhaka is very close by...

My wife's name is Asma Begum. She is 20 years old. She has long, black hair and black eyes. She wears pink sari and pink scarf. She cry because I go away to UK.

19th February 2005

Dear Asma,

Today strange thing happened. I was walking down street when I see footpath green in colour. I look close by and see small small small pieces of glass. Full street covered. I stand and look. So pretty they look. Shining in the sun. Yesterday Wales winning rugby match against France. People going mad. I can see stadium from my house. Big stadium with big arms sticking out in the sky, like monster spider. I hear shouts and singing from inside. Like how we can hear shouting from Dhanmondi Stadium when cricket match is on. I remember sitting outside stadium with transistor and cigarettes, shouting with the crowd inside. Here people celebrating with beer all night. And they breaking bottles on the road, I don't know why. Maybe celebration tradition like that. I don't know how to play rugby, so I ask man from Somalia who sit next to me in class. He not knowing also and he live in UK four years. He saying it is all fighting on the field. So I watch on TV highlights and get headache. Too much *dishum-dishum*, little bit playing. I not understanding. Here no cricket on TV or on radio. Muyazzumbhai call Bangladesh every ten minutes to know score. He having too much money to spend.

Do you watch cricket match with Abba and Ammi? When I go home next time, we will go to stadium and see live cricket, okay?

Hassan

Would you like to give the order, sir? What would you like to drink? Mineral water, fizzy or still? Anything else? Thank you, sir, will that be all? Do come again, goodnight.

5th March 2005

Dear Asma,

How are you? Why you getting headache? What the doctor said? Is everything okay? I call you on Saturday. You go to Lucky telephone booth, 7 p.m. I call you. Say you going to market or something, and then I don't have to talk to Ammi and Abba. You take care of baby, okay? Do not feel sad. I tell you a new story now. Maybe you smile.

Customers in Royal B.C. like the food. Yesterday Rafiqmia made mistake and gave too hot too spicy food to *gora* man yesterday. His face turning red like beetroot and he cough coughing. He saying bad words to waiter from Syria, his name Ivan and throw curry on the floor. His friend laughing all the time. They both shouting loud and banging on table. They say they complain and close down restaurant. Muyazzumbhai gave free dinner to them, but when they go out, they wink and show middle finger and run. I not understanding these people. They go to pub and drink. Then they come for curry again, but man with beetroot face vomit on table. Muyazzumbhai call police. They run away and now we have to give policemen free curry. Takeaway.

I have. You have. He has. She has. It has. They have. We have. I haven't. You haven't. He hasn't. They haven't. We haven't.

25th March 2005

Dear Asma,

I am so happy today. God is good to us. You take care of yourself. You haven't written to me. I'll pray for a healthy baby. You must not do too much work. No heavy-duty work. Sleep in the afternoon. Next month, I'll ask Ammi to send you to your Ammi's house, okay? I'll send you money soon.

I had exams today. Speaking and listening. One teacher came from London, and she asked me questions. I can say all the answers, very easy like. Then I have to ask her questions. Her name is Siân. I say it is man's name in Bangladesh. I ask her to spell, but it is something else only. S-I-A-N. Shaan. I think nice name for boy, innit? But no good. When you come to Cardiff, people will laugh and say you give boy a girl's name. I asked her if she is married. She said no, she isn't. Then I make big mistake. I ask her if she has children. I bite my tongue. I'm sure I fail now. She says yes, a boy. I bite my tongue again. She's not good lady. But man from Somalia say many women here not married and have children. He know this because he been here four years. When you come here, you not speak to such ladies. Then Betty-teacher say she has partner, not husband and I'm sad. She's such a nice lady. I tell her you have baby soon, *insha-allah*. Betty teacher very happy for me and she say, congratulations. Like when passing exams. I am very happy and proud man today. My Asma having baby soon.

Love,
Hassan

Baby – babies   lady-ladies   man-men   woman-women child-children

9th May 2005

Dear lovely wife,

I am happy you are in your mother's house. Take rest there. Tell your Ammi to make chicken soup for you. Very good. I will try and send you chicken soup from here. Rafiqmia is going to Bangladesh. I will send you Baxters soup. I will buy from Tesco. You know, from supermarket, very very big shop. Maybe big like football stadium. When I go there, I am nervous. So many things I see, I forget what to buy. When I think of Rehana stores in Dhaka, I laugh. It is smaller than one aisle in Tesco. And Tesco not just one supermarket. Sainsbury's, Asda, Lidl, ... more, more, more. My head go round and round when I see so many things. So much food. From where they come? From Kenya, Argentina, Spain, from far far away. I want to eat *muri*, but cannot find in any of these supermarkets. I go to tiny Bangladeshi shop in Clare Road, and there I find my food. *Muri, daal, ilish maach* – frozen of course. But I hear you cannot eat fish any more. Not liking smell? So now I will not eat *ilish maach* also. It is cheaper here than at home.

I buy some baby clothes. I know you will say bad luck to buy before baby comes, but what to do? Now special price, buy one get one free. I also buy, no, bought nappies. Pampers. Don't get angry. I will keep in Champa-*mashi's* house if you want. Please send me photo of what you are looking like now. Champa-*mashi's* daughter-in-law having baby also. And her son have photo of baby inside stomach. I cannot believe it. Then he showed me, and I think, this like E.T., that *bhoot* in the film. He get very angry. What to do, better not to see what you not supposed to see. I only see my baby when he coming out, not like *bhoot* inside tummy.

Write soon,

Hassan

I'm sorry but I have a bit of a problem... I'm afraid that... Please could I have my money back?... If you don't mind... Please can I exchange this for a larger size?...

1st June 2005

Dearest,

It was raining today and I ~~go~~ went inside a bus-stop. Here bus-stop has roof and bench to sit on. And bus come and go like trains in Dhaka – with a timetable. Many people sitting inside. All talking about rain. How hard is raining. They saying 'tipping it'. I look at sky and suddenly I laugh. I laugh and laugh, and people scared of me. They move far away. But I look at the rain and think, in Bangladesh when the roofs fly, we complain about the rain. Here umbrella fly and people are worried.

But it is good here. At least umbrella fly. Big umbrella cost £2.99. There roof fly, cannot buy new roof. No money. But don't worry, I send money to Abbajan for repair on roof. No more plastic sheet on top of kitchen roof.

I watch on TV, floods in England. Very bad situation. But everything so good, every person is getting bottled water from government and helicopter come to save

people and their cats and dogs. I say what a great country. In Bangladesh, when floods come, we drink cholera water and pick up dead babies from water with our hands. What a lucky country this... our son must grow up here. You will come here soon.
Hassan

Mustafa is Somali. Asif is Pakistani. Maria is Polish. Hassan is Bangladeshi. Abdullah is Afghani. Li Jian is Korean. Nao is Japanese. Ahmed is Iraqi. Bahaar is Kurdish... the bombers are Muslim.

20th July, 2005

Dear Asma,
The bombers were Mussalman. Just like that. What is their country? Doesn't matter. What is their language? Doesn't matter. They are Muslim – that matters. I know now all Muslims can be terrorists. I'm afraid to go out. *I'm sorry I have a bit of a problem* – I'm Muslim. The terrorists bombed the station in London on July 7th. And you know what? Muyazzumbhai was in London that day. And you know what? He never come back. He was the bomber? Or the victim? How do we know, because he is Muslim? What do we tell his wife and sons? Will his sons, so sweet young boys become terrorists to revenge for their father? Now I walk the long street in shame. I'm not ever looking up. Some boys here, shout Bin Laden when I pass by. They spit and laugh and run. I want to cry. Bin Laden kill my Muyazzumbhai. Do I look like terrorist? I shave my beard and moustache, even if it was Amitabh Bachchan style. I too scared to watch TV.

Maybe I hear Muyazzumbhai is terrorist. Cannot trust anyone.

In school also, very quiet. People very scared... and ashamed. Muslim people very quiet. Betty teacher look sad, but she try to make us smile. But we too ashamed. I say sorry to her, on behalf of all Muslim people. She started to cry. Her friend also, killed in train. She say 'senseless massacre'. She say 'insane people'. She say 'threat to mankind'. I cannot understand big words but I know they are bad words. I feel terrible. I feel I am the terrorist who kill her friend. I will never go back to school again. But if I don't, they think I am terrorist and come to find me. What do I do? I am not free man any more.

Am I threat to UK? I don't know. I have a wife who wore pink sari to airport and cried when I went. She is pregnant. So what? Bomber was assistant teacher in school and he had family. He was Muslim, like me. Am I a terrorist because I pray five times a day? I hide from the mirror. I learn a new word – *coward*. I have no job now. Royal B.C. is closed. It is now Polish supermarket called Ziomek. My classmate, Sylvester, working there now. He looked at me but not smile. Another coward. Do I want my son to be in this country? Maybe not. I don't know. In this country supermarket so big, is bigger than our railway station, I think. He will never be hungry. But he will never be proud man, always ashamed.

I know on those trains bombed, there were English, Polish, Italian, Welsh, Somali, Arabic, Indian, Pakistani, Bangladeshi... and one terrorist with a bomb in his bag.

Did he say 'goodbye' to the passengers before he push the button? And in which language?

Goodbye, my dear,

Hassan

Do widzenia.   Ciao.   Hwyl.   Nabad gelyo.   Ma'a salama. Namaste.   Khuda hafiz.

Biographies

John Abell
John Abell was born in Cardiff in 1986 and has lived throughout Wales and the south of England. He allegedly studied at Camberwell but spent much of his time in Soho bars. John is a prolific artist and has won many awards, most recently winning the printmaking and overall runner up prizes at Welsh Artist of the Year 2013. http://johnabell.blogspot.co.uk

Lane Ashfeldt
Lane Ashfeldt's stories can be read online at the *Guardian*, *Southword* literary journal, *The View From Here* and *Identity Theory*. Ashfeldt grew up between Dublin and London, and currently lives in a small town in Powys. A sense of wider landscapes and the natural world is a recurrent theme in her writing, which has won

several awards. A collection, *SaltWater*, will be published in 2014. @Ashfeldt

Susmita Bhattacharya

Susmita Bhattacharya was born in Mumbai, India. She sailed around the world in an oil tanker for three years with her husband, recording her voyages through painting and writing journals. She received an MA in Creative Writing from Cardiff University in 2006 and has had several short stories and poems published since. She lives in Plymouth with her husband, two daughters and the neighbour's cat. Her debut novel, *Crossing Borders*, will be published by Parthian Books in 2014. @Susmitatweets http://susmita-bhattacharya.blogspot.co.uk

Sarah Coles

Sarah Coles lives in Swansea. Her poetry collection, *Here and the Water*, was recently published by Gomer. She is currently working on a collection of short stories.

Siân Melangell Dafydd

Author, poet and translator, Siân Melangell Dafydd's first published novel, *Y Trydydd Peth* (*The Third Thing*; Gomer, 2009) won her the coveted 2009 National Eisteddfod Literature Medal. She writes in both Welsh and English and often collaborates with artists of other disciplines (dancer Sioned Huws' *Aomori Project;* book *Ancestral Houses: the Lost Mansions of Wales/Tai Mawr a Mieri: Plastai Coll Cymru* with poet Damian Walford Davies and artist Paul White [Gomer 2012]). She is the co-editor of the literary review, *Taliesin*, and *Y Neuadd* online literary magazine which nurtures new voices. Her second Welsh-language novel is to be published by Gomer in 2014.

Deborah Kay Davies
Deborah Kay Davies's first collection of stories, *Grace, Tamar and Laszlo the Beautiful* (Parthian Books) won the Wales Book of the Year award in 2009. When her first novel, *True Things About Me* (Canongate Books), came out in 2010 Deborah was named on BBC TV's *Culture Show* as one of the twelve best new British novelists. And when the novel was published in the States by Faber and Faber, Lionel Shriver made it her personal Book of the Year. Her new novel, *Reasons She Goes To The Woods*, will be published by Oneworld in 2014.

Rhian Edwards
Rhian's first collection of poems *Clueless Dogs* (Seren) recently won Wales Book of the Year 2013, the Roland Mathias Prize for Poetry 2013 and the Wales People's Choice 2013 as well as being shortlisted for the Forward Prize for Best First Collection 2012. Rhian's poems and flash fictions have featured in the *Guardian*, *Times Literary Supplement*, *Poetry Review*, *Arete*, *the Spectator*, *Poetry London*, *Poetry Wales*, *Prague Revue*, *the London Magazine*, *Stand*, *Planet Magazine*, *New Welsh Review* and *The Lampeter Review*. http://rhianedwards.co.uk

Roshi Fernando
Roshi Fernando was born and brought up in London and holds a PhD in Creative Writing at the University

of Wales, Swansea. In 2009 she was awarded the Impress Prize for New Writers, for her composite novel, *Homesick*, which comprises a series of interlinked short stories about a community of Sri Lankan immigrants in London, published by Bloomsbury. In 2011 her story 'The Fluorescent Jacket' was shortlisted for the EFG *Sunday Times* short story prize. She is currently working on a novel and a collection of short stories. Roshi lives in Gloucestershire with her partner and four children.

Eluned Gramich
Eluned Gramich was born in west Wales and grew up speaking Welsh and German. She studied English at Oxford before completing the UEA Creative Writing MA. Eluned currently lives and works in Japan, where she is also translating Monique Schwitter's full short story collection *Goldfischgedächtnis* for Parthian and working on her own first novel. She was shortlisted for the Bristol Short Story Prize 2011.

Craig Hawes
Craig Hawes grew up in Briton Ferry, south Wales. He has worked as a journalist in London and Dubai, where he currently lives. He was shortlisted for the Bristol Short Story Prize 2009, was runner-up in the Rhys Davies Prize 2010, and placed third in the Yeovil Short Story Prize, 2010. Hawes' short stories have appeared in several publications and prize-winning anthologies including *Blue Tattoo*, Bristol Prize Anthology in 2009. He has also had stories and an afternoon play broadcast

on BBC Radio 4. Craig's debut collection of short stories is *The Witch Doctor of Umm Suqeim* (Parthian, 2013).

Carly Holmes

Carly is in the final year of a Creative Writing PhD. She's had a number of short stories shortlisted in competitions and published in journals, and her debut novel, *The Scrapbook*, is forthcoming (Parthian, 2014). Carly organises The Cellar Bards, a group of writers who meet in Cardigan monthly for a lively evening of spoken word, and she's also on the editorial board of *The Lampeter Review*. When not doing any of the above, Carly can usually be found in her garden, talking to her hedge sparrows.

Tyler Keevil

Tyler Keevil was born in Edmonton and grew up in Vancouver, Canada. His short fiction has been widely published, and has earned him several awards, including 1st Prize in the Frome Festival International Story Competition for 'Mangleface'. Parthian recently released his debut novel, *Fireball*, which was longlisted for Wales Book of the Year, shortlisted for the *Guardian* Not the Booker prize, and received the Media Wales People's Prize 2011. His second novel, *The Drive*, was published in 2013. His debut collection of short fiction, *Burrard Inlet* is published by Parthian in 2014. He lectures in creative writing at the University of Gloucestershire, and lives in mid Wales with his wife and son.

Peter Krištúfek
Peter Krištúfek was born in 1973 and grew up in Bratislava, Slovakia. He has an MA in Film and Television Directing from the Academy of Performing Arts, Bratislava, and is an award-winning director. His writing has appeared in numerous Slovak and foreign anthologies, including the annual anthology, *Best European Fiction 2010*, and many Slovak newspapers and magazines. Peter's third novel, *The House of the Deaf Man*, is out in translation through Parthian in 2014.

Robert Lewis
Robert Lewis is a writer from Abergavenny who has published three novels and one work of non-fiction. He can very occasionally be seen reading short stories in Cardiff bars.

John Minahane
John Minahane is from Ireland and has lived in Bratislava since 1996. Books translated by him include: Ladislav Novomeskı, *Slovak Spring* (Belfast 2004); Milan Rúfus, *To Bear The Burden And Sing* (Martin 2008); *Six Slovak Poets*, ed. Igor Hochel (Todmorden, UK 2008); Emire Khidayer, *Tales from Sumhuram* (e-book, 2012).

Joâo Morais
Joâo Morais recently won the 2013 Terry Hetherington Young Writer's Award. A nominee for the 2009 Rhys Davies Short Story Prize, he was also shortlisted for the 2013 Percy French Prize for Comic Verse. He is currently studying for a PhD in creative writing at Cardiff University.

Holly Müller
Holly Müller is a Cardiff-based writer and tutor of creative writing at the University of Glamorgan. Holly is working on her first novel, a historical fiction work set in post-war Austria.

Rebbecca Ray
Rebbecca Ray is the author of *A Certain Age*, *Newfoundland* and *The Answer and Other Love Stories*. She lives in mid Wales with her growing family.

Richard Owain Roberts
Richard Owain Roberts has had short stories published in print and across the internet. He lives in Cardiff, Wales, with his wife and cat. Follow @RichOwainRobs.

Monique Schwitter
Monique Schwitter was born in 1972 in Zürich, and has been living in Hamburg, Germany since 2005. She studied Drama and Directing in Salzburg and has worked at various theatres in Zürich, Frankfurt, Graz and Hamburg among others. She now lives as a freelance author in Hamburg. She received the Robert-Walser Prize and the Förderpreis der Schweizer Schillerstiftung (2006) for her debut work, *Wenn's schneit beim Krokodil* (2005). Her novel *Ohren haben keine Lider* was published in 2008, and her recent collection of short-stories *Goldfischgedächtnis* was awarded the Rotahornpreis in 2011.

Rachel Trezise

Rachel Trezise was born in south Wales in 1978. Her semi-autobiographical novel *In and Out of the Goldfish Bowl* was published by Parthian in 2000, to critical acclaim and a place on the Orange Futures List. Her short story collection *Fresh Apples*, won the inaugural Dylan Thomas Prize in 2006. *Dial M for Merthyr* won the inaugural Max Boyce Prize in 2010. Her most recent book is *Cosmic Latte* (Parthian, 2013). Her work has been translated into several languages and published all over the world. Her first full-length play *Tonypandemonium* was produced by National Theatre Wales in 2013.

Dan Tyte

Dan Tyte was born 32 years ago in Splott, Cardiff. Since then, he's interviewed rock stars, ghost-written *Guardian* features, become a *Western Mail* columnist and written *Half Plus Seven*, his debut novel out with Parthian in Spring 2014. www.dantyte.com

Susie Wild

Susie Wild is the Editor at Parthian. Her debut collection of short stories *The Art of Contraception* was longlisted for the Edge Hill Short Story Prize. She is the literary programmer for Do Not Go Gentle Festival in Swansea and a co-organiser of xx women's writing festival held at Chapter Arts Centre. She currently lives in Cardiff, where she is working on her second collection of stories and a novel. @Soozerama

Georgia Carys Williams

Georgia Carys Williams was born in Swansea. She won third prize at the Terry Hetherington Award 2012, highly commended for The south Wales Short Story Competition 2012 and was shortlisted for the Swansea Life Young Writing Category of the Dylan Thomas Prize, 2008. Whilst working on a PhD in Creative Writing at Swansea University, she writes for *Wales Arts Review*. Her debut short story collection will be published by Parthian in 2014.

Acknowledgements

'The Battle of St Mary Street' by Robert Lewis was originally performed at In Chapters in Cardiff.

'Holiday of a Lifetime' by Rachel Trezise is taken from her second collection of short stories, *Cosmic Latte* (Parthian, 2013).

'Mangleface' by Tyler Keevil won 1st Prize in the Frome Festival International Story Competition, and is a preview from his forthcoming collection of short stories *Burrard Inlet* (Parthian, 2014).

'The Bereaved' by Georgia Carys Williams is a preview from her forthcoming collection of short stories *Second-hand Rain* (Parthian, 2014).

'Sound Waves' by Lane Ashfeldt features in her debut collection of short stories *SaltWater*, self-published in 2013.

'Keeper' by Rebbecca Ray is taken from her debut collection of short stories *The Answer & Other Love Stories* (Parthian, 2013).

'Into the Inwood' by Rhian Edwards was originally written and performed for Imagistic in Swansea.

'Moles' by Monique Schwitter is a translation of 'Male' from her collection of stories *Goldfischgedächtnis*.